CW00521712

ADVENTURES IN OPPOSITE LAND

THE MEMOIR SHORTS
VOLUME 1

Randy Zinn

SOR Press
GAITHERSBURG, MARYLAND

Randy Zinn/SOR Press
Gaithersburg, Maryland
www.randy-zinn.com

Publisher's Note: Any names, characters, or places have been changed to protect anonymity. Any resemblance to actual people, living or dead, or to businesses, companies, events, institutions, or locales is coincidental.

Adventures in Opposite Land / Randy Zinn. -- 1st ed.
ISBN 978-1-9536431-1-7 (paperback)
ISBN 978-1-9536431-4-8 (hardcover)

Contents

ACKNOWLEDGEMENTS

Special thanks to Logan Russell and Daniela Zorrilla

Cover design by JD&J Design

Preface

Thank you for opening my memoir! I have a few notes before we get started.

Men are not known for keeping a diary, but I have since 1990 due to the terrible turmoil that marked my teens and twenties. I've kept doing it ever since, chronicling my life even when I didn't need to work out my distress in its pages. The events recounted herein are a combination of my memory and the sometimes minute detail of my biweekly diary. It has allowed me to render this story with a high degree of accuracy.

This book is a collection of stories that don't need to be read in a particular order and are not presented chronologically. Here is a quick rundown of the tales.

"All That Remains" takes place in 1996 and is the story of my first post-college job, where I had my first major encounter with office politics.

"Karma Delivered" is about my first job after high school as a truck loader for Parcel Fast, where I first began to learn that hard work and diligence may not only fail to cause recognition at work, but can cost us our job.

"The Stand Up" is a very short story about an interesting excuse I was giving for being stood up on a date.

In "White Rocks," the homeowner's association of my community set in motion foreclosing on my home and evicting me and my wife, and they weren't even going to tell us why. The reason was a stunner, as was the way they were handling it.

In 2019, "I'm Open to Suggestions" details an altercation with an event planner on Meetup.com and her take on what makes an effective host.

That same year, a dream vacation to New Zealand had some unwelcome drama between me and another trip-goer, detailed in "The Dark Whisperer," a story of intentions, assumptions, and the hell found in between.

All names, including those of some businesses, have been changed for privacy. There are no composite characters. I eventually changed my first name to Randy, with most calling me Rand; these stories span periods before and after that, and I just used this name for all stories regardless of when they happened.

Free Book

A free eBook is available to newsletter subscribers.

All That Remains

While many of us see no value in discarded things—whether items, places, or even people—some of us are drawn to them. We can only hope to be viewed this way if we are the disposed item. Humankind has a long history of declaring such persons worthless. This idea is offensive but can be familiar from social groups, personal relationships, and jobs. Sometimes we see the rejection coming, but we may be too busy hoping for the best to see the worst barreling toward us, and I was one such blind person at my first job after college.

Icarus Books was a place that loved discarded items. In their case, it wasn't for love or sentiment, but profit. When book publishers stop trying to sell a title, they typically have many unsold printed copies lying around. These "remaindered" books could number in the dozens or thousands. Not wanting to destroy them but unable to give them away, publishers did the next best thing—they sold them en masse for pennies on the dollar at auction.

And that was where Icarus Books came in, snatching them up to sell cheap books to the public. They had been doing this since the early 1980s, long before Al Gore invented the internet in the mid-1990s, so they were still doing business the old-fashioned way. They had a catalogue they mailed once a quarter, and interested customers called into the customer service center to order what they wanted. And one person answering the phone was yours truly.

I had struggled with speech problems since I was eight years old, but the issue most people noticed was that I mumbled. However, I never did it on the phone. I cannot be certain why, but I had long suspected that, with no visual cues, people are less likely to interrupt on the phone, and relentless interruption by my family had triggered the psychological problems that led to speech issues. Ultimately, I could speak clearly on the phone but in no other context, and so rather than being leery of such a job, I felt attracted to it; another memoir, *Refusal to Engage*, details the speech troubles.

Fresh off my Bachelor of Music degree in classical guitar in 1995, I very much needed a break from college before returning for a master's degree. Five years of hell had also worn me out (discussed in my memoir, *A Blast of Light*). I just wanted a simple life, writing music and stories at home when not at a peaceful job, which I hoped would be more fulfilling than making sandwiches or loading trucks as I had done before. Since I was also an author, Icarus Books appealed to me and I became an employee in late 1995. While I wanted a full-time job and benefits, they hired everyone part-time at thirty hours a week for a month or two as a kind of probation, after which you became full-time. Close enough.

Icarus Books had an old warehouse near College Park, Maryland, with an empty gravel lot providing unmarked parking and no reserved spaces. The red-brick building was two stories, but the first was a loading bay I never saw the interior of as I climbed steel steps to the second floor and a hall. To the left, through the doors, was a large open room with row upon row of tables, each with books stacked on them, the infrequently placed fluorescent lights making it seem gloomy. The floor in there had the occasional ramp; one staff member talked fondly of her days wearing roller skates on the job, racing around the room to pull books for an order, before they moved her from Fulfillment to Customer Service, which was across the hall.

That was where I worked with the other Customer Service Reps (CSRs). On stepping into the open room, to the right on the same wall with the door were two workstations. To the left was a supply cabinet and a lone workstation for the Customer Relations person. This was the lone person who dealt with serious customer and order problems and didn't take orders like the rest of us unless we were swamped. The entire right wall held four more workstations, but the left one only had two, for the new hires, because in front of that was the massive work area of our manager, Jane, who had a perpetually cluttered desk and several equally overflowing tables around her. This was all up against the far wall with the only other door, which led to the HR office and a hallway, at the end of which were the company owners. The CSRs were under strict orders to never set foot anywhere but our room, the bathroom, or the break room, but I eventually saw it all.

Since new hires needed her help, they had to sit by Jane before graduating to somewhere else in the room. Officially, no one but Customer Relations had an assigned desk, but people are creatures of habit and typically took the same one each day. The full-timers worked 9-5, except for one, who came in at 2pm and stayed until 10pm, acting as a kind of supervisor for the night shift, who were the only people expected to always be part-time. For day-shift new hires starting at part-time, we started with everyone else and just left after six hours.

Jane was jovial and good-natured, with a quick smile and a hearty laugh that made her instantly likeable. She fostered a positive, cooperative atmosphere and politely asked people to do one thing or another even though she could have rudely commanded it, but that wasn't her personality. She accentuated her girth (I assume inadvertently) by wearing tight-fitting, blue sweatpants and a matching top every day, each with a hole or two. She went without makeup and left her long black hair, streaked with gray, in a loose, unwashed cascade around her shoulders.

Whereas Jane did little to cast an air of authority and stern disapproval, one full-timer took that role. Mark was a humorless little mustached man who acted very proper, always casting a frown at me and a few others of my ilk for our irreverent sense of humor. He seemed to think socializing was unacceptable, and so if any of us were talking amongst ourselves during a time with few phone calls coming in, he was quick to hush someone. And yes, he was the sort to use the word "hush."

Despite this, he was likeable in his own dour way, and I mostly mention him because his departure set in motion my troubles, for two reasons. The first is that, had he still been there, he would have quickly snuffed the office politics that arose and took over the room, whereas Jane let them fester. The second was that I took over a job function that he had been responsible for, and that work set the politics in motion.

Except for that additional function, all the CSRs had the same job. A batch of mail-in order forms always awaited us and had been grouped into piles of fifty, a rubber band around them. These sat in a wicker basket on a table in the room's center behind Jane, who sat with her back to us. When we were not on the phone, we entered these orders into the computer system. If the phone rang, we answered it, then returned to the mail order after. A customer was typically calling to place an order we also entered. That was the job. By 1 or 2pm, the mail orders were usually done, and if you finished your initial pile early, you grabbed another, but there were seldom enough for this to be needed. And if the phones were quiet, you had little to do except read a book.

And they required us to do this. From each quarterly catalogue, we needed to choose five books to read. Then we had to give a verbal book report on all five to the rest of the CSRs, including those from the night shift who came in early for this long meeting. It always took place before they sent the next catalogue. The reason was so that we could upsell. When a customer called to order a book, we needed to know what similar books we were selling and try to talk them into buying them. This was the part of the job none of us liked, and everyone knew it, including the company Chief Operating Officer, Ellen.

She was in her mid-40s, perpetually dour faced (her and Mark should have had babies), and was tall, skinny, and had dark blonde, curly, frizzy hair that made her seem several inches taller. No one had ever seen her smile, not to mention laugh, and she always seemed like she had just eaten something distasteful. She wore square glasses low on her nose and looked over them at you with an air of disapproval. If she walked into the room, any chatter died instantly, because she was all business and the sort to walk right up to you and bluntly challenge you as to why you didn't have any work to do. The phone not ringing, no mail orders being available to process, and you having finished your five chosen books weren't good excuses because she would unceremoniously hand you another book to read. She seemed to think she was paying you to do nothing in those unproductive moments, and while that was technically true, she showed no awareness that a little downtime was good for morale. It was also hardly your fault that the phone wasn't ringing and the mail orders were all processed. You weren't screwing her over; you had done your job.

Maybe all of this was why Mark acted sternly toward us. Was he trying to prevent Ellen, who always entered without warning, from disapproving of the room? He came across like a protective father trying to prevent his kids from getting in trouble with the school principal.

One of Ellen's most infamous, oft-repeated acts was to walk up behind you while you were talking to a customer on the phone, blatantly looking over your shoulder at the order and listening to your part of the conversation. She wanted to know if you were upselling, something she pushed hard for. God help us all if she didn't hear you do it, or if you didn't seem to try hard enough in her mind, or if you simply failed to increase the order. Ellen would accost you the moment you hung up, or chastise the entire room, all of us knowing she was doing it because of you, as if she was blatantly shaming you to the rest of us and trying to make everyone hate you because you had caused it. This time. Eventually, pretty much everyone got "the treatment." We all felt the horrible pressure of it, well aware this woman could fire us.

Sometimes she would snap, "Jane, to my office," and we knew what was happening because Jane would come back, looking like she'd seen a ghost, and implore all of us to upsell. This occurred often enough that Ellefson was doing it again, and making it clear that one of us had essentially gotten our manager lectured. Naturally, this could have been terrible for any of us, but we all hated Ellen, including Jane (she never would have admitted it), and thought she was over-the-top, unreasonable, and cruel. Rather than any of us hating on the CSR who had caused it this time, we all sympathized with each other for Ellen's attempt to single us out. Other times, rather than Ellen berating Jane in private, she did it right in front of us, showing no respect for not making Jane look bad in front of her staff.

Ellen was a straight-up bitch.

But I got on her good side one day when I discovered an error in the manufacturing of CDs that we had 2,000 copies of and were trying to sell. I told Jane, who told Ellen, who told the record company. Even they hadn't known about it and had to recall all of them. I had saved the company a lot of money by preventing us from selling a problematic product. Ellen was thrilled—it was the only time any of us had ever seen her smile—and I soon received a performance review with a raise and positive comments about getting along with people.

But it didn't last. I was reviewing the music marketing materials, too, and pointed out some mistakes in them, having no idea that Ellen was responsible for those errors. She actually seemed amused when informing me that since I was so smart, that I could write all of them myself from now on. I think she was pleased that I had avoided the company looking bad, but I had also shown her up, a fact that had my peers smirking that I was going to get myself fired. People seemed to respect these moments from me, but nothing lasts forever.

With Mark's departure, I became the only CSR who understood the few classical music CDs we were also selling, though we also had some jazz ones. Before they hired me, if a customer had a question about the CDs, the CSR had to put them on hold and go talk to Mark, and sometimes even transfer the order to him to complete, because it was better for a customer to chat with a fellow enthusiast of the genre than a sales rep who did not know. The CSRs could have done this with me, too, but they didn't until Mark quit. That's when they overheard me fielding customer questions about the music, and the difference be-

tween ADD, DDD, and similar labels on CDs; these referred to the analog and digital nature of the recordings.
Now the CSRs came to me, but sometimes I was on the
phone already and couldn't get off. This prompted me to
suggest that I do the CD version of the book reports so that
staff could handle it themselves. While we all had to review and report on five books in a catalogue, I would now
have to do thirty CDs. They agreed.

As expected, those who were to advance to full-time
did so in the order they were hired, and I was the second
in line. This process sometimes sped up when a full-timer
quit, but as the new year began, several of them left the
company and yet no word came of a change. They did not
promote the girl ahead of me. I asked Jane about this and
she told me to see Ashley, the lone HR person.

"No one is going full time anymore," Ashley advised
me, sitting behind her desk, the only clean one I had seen
at the company. Ashley was a big black woman who had
that mix of helpfulness and distance that HR reps often
have. These are the people who help you come on board,
but they are also the ones to let people go, and she walked
the line of being pleasant but ready to do her unsavory
duties when needed. Now was time for the latter.

"What?" I asked in surprise, unhappy. "Why?"

She shrugged. "They've just made a change and prefer
having more part-timers. We're phasing out almost all full-
time staff, replacing them with part-timers when someone
leaves."

"Yeah, but you agreed to bring me on full-time."

"Well, that was then. This is now."

I wondered if this was a breach of contract but wasn't
sure how to ask, aware of her power to terminate me. I had
also noticed that no one bothered to tell me this, just leaving me hanging until I said something. But I only remarked,

"I've been counting on this going full-time. I need the hours, money, and benefits."

"Well, if it's a problem, the only thing you can do is leave."

I frowned, put off even more. Just because it was true, didn't mean she should float the idea of me leaving. Coming from an HR rep, that was especially concerning. Were they thinking to ditch me? Or was I now volunteering myself to be removed as a potentially unhappy staff member? There wasn't much more I could say to that and soon left, considering whether to work somewhere else, but I liked my job. Taking the orders was easy, the mood of the room suited me, and several of my coworkers shared my sensibilities and humor so that it sometimes felt like I was hanging out more than working. This usually happened later in the day when the mail orders were done and the phone calls slowed.

A skinny black girl named Dee always knew I appreciated something silly or irreverent, and would bring such things to my attention. This was true whether she had seen it in a book we sold, I missed a remark while on the phone, or a customer said something interesting to her. A sassy redhead named Leanne fulfilled the role of matriarch because this was her only job, going on fifteen years back to when the company formed. As a result, she had worked every position and wasn't the manager in Jane's role because she didn't want to be. She looked out for us and sometimes disapproved, but she knew who did well at their job so that once you had her approval, she joked with you more.

I was also thinking about returning to college, and a part-time job made that easier than a full-time one. Maybe I would stick around, but I had intended to go back to school for my masters in music all along, and having a part-time job like this seemed like a good idea.

Me and the other CSR that had been in line for full-time had been removed from our seats next to Jane to make way for new hires Derek and Karen. With their arrival and the departure of Mark, trouble was brewing.

Derek was tall, lanky, and wore a full, thin brown beard to go with his medium-length, wavy brown hair, which he parted on one side. He seemed disingenuous from the start, showing only passing interest in what someone else said, as if he was doing the bare minimum to ingratiate himself with you but slowly making it clear he didn't really care. He could be a little funny but tended toward being snide, and yet he made his cutting remarks casually, in a laid-back style, which was how he seemed to do everything. For reasons I still don't understand, he immediately became Jane's darling, so much so that when his time as a newbie ended and they should have moved him from there to make way for other new hires, it became an almost officially assigned seat. I wondered how he was achieving this, for he was slightly repellent. Some of us joked they were having an affair.

Karen was short, blonde, athletic, and aggressive, both in how she moved and with her judgments and language. Her black-and-white worldview made her confrontational and gave her a chip on her shoulder that made her willing to start something with someone else, which increasingly became me. She was the sort to first fabricate an issue and then pick a fight over it, finding reasons to cause arguments, usually over something petty. For example, she liked to claim ownership of something, whether it be a desk or parking space, trying to forbid and intimidate someone from her falsely claimed territories. "You took my spot!" was a frequent immature accusation. I hated her immediately, and the feeling was mutual. In time I was her Chosen Enemy.

By now I was reviewing the CDs and writing marketing materials, but it was hard for me to keep up. One day, Ellen came directly to my cube while Jane wasn't in the room and pointed out that the number of orders I entered had dropped. When I said the CD work was the reason, she told me that was no excuse and that they expected me to do the additional duties even though there wasn't time. I said I could always stay late to do them and she just walked away.

The next day, Ashley in HR called me into a meeting and asked, "Did you ask Ellen for full-time hours the other day?"

Startled, I asked, "What? No. Why would you think that?"

"She said you asked for more hours to do the CD work."

"Well, I did," I mumbled, "but I meant just to get that done, not forever, and it's because I can't get them done and do my other work and she was giving me a hard time about it."

She glared at me and snapped, "It is not appropriate to go over Jane's head like that. All of us are furious with you."

Being told your manager, HR Director, and the Chief Operating Officer at your employer feel that way about you is always alarming, and more so when you are younger. I felt shocked at the false accusation and a little speechless. This was Ellen's doing. She did not misunderstand my intent and mischaracterized the conversation to Jane and Ashley, who took her word for it. Part of me wanted to say something to Jane to clear it up, but such a conversation had to happen in front of the entire room; I had once asked to talk to her privately about something and been told no. Concern that my manager, who I quite liked, now disliked me made me watch for signs of disapproval, but I did not

see them. Jane gave the impression that she would cheer-
fully smile and not show it, however, so I did not feel com-
forted.

Shortly after this, I noticed that there wasn't a master
list of CDs we sold and offered to Jane to create one. I received no response, but days later, Leanne, the matriarch
of the room, announced she was throwing out all the old
catalogues before the week was over and that I had better
take them now to make the list from them. I started typing
up the list, a little each day when all my mail orders were
done and the phone wasn't ringing.

Then I was once again called into HR and reamed out
by Ashley. Apparently, Jane had taken my suggestion to
Ellen, who had agreed and started making the list herself,
and when Ellen learned I was making one, she decided I
was trying to show her up. She was furious. Ashley ordered me to never show any initiative again despite me
being the one who had given the idea to Ellen, and my initiative having already saved the company a lot of money
about those bad CDs. This angered me for several reasons,
including what I saw as punishing me for trying to help.
Didn't they want an employee who gave a damn? Now I
cared a little less and resented my good work getting me
singled out as a bad staff member. Indignation had me trying to keep a scowl of disapproval from my face. Maybe
this wasn't a good place to work after all. Jane now
frowned at me more often than before, giving the impression her opinion of me had fallen.

I thought Ellen was insecure and petty, easily threatened by someone who had no power. I also suspected that
Jane had told Ellen the CD master list idea and made it
sound like it was her plan, but with me making the list
now, I inadvertently made it clear that the idea was once
again mine, ruining her lie and embarrassing her. It now
seemed like every good intention was just paving my road

to hell. I began to dislike my job and feel contempt for management, but at least Leanne, who had been about to trash the old catalogues, and who suggested I make the list from them first, apologized for her part in instigating me to do it.

By now, Derek had changed the room's dynamics, with help from Karen. The room design meant all of us had a desk attached to the wall, a small, cubicle-like wall separating us before and behind. The side facing the room was fully open, allowing us to see half of the others. We slowly noticed that, when the phone rang, Derek would not pick it up. Instead, he would look across the room to see if someone else was going to get it so that he didn't have to. We all resented him doing this and complained to Jane more than once, but since Derek was her pet, she would chastise us to grow up. Derek's monitoring became contagious as all of us began watching how much work each other appeared to be doing. This often meant the phone continued to ring, no one getting it.

Hearing the phone still ringing, Jane would sometimes turn around with an inquisitive look, because she was a backup who took orders when she had to, since that was better than letting an order get away if the person never called back. Due to her physical position, she could see all of us, but with only the two newbies, including her pet Derek, to her left, she turned right to look at the rest of us. And most of us would see this, and one of us would resentfully answer, only to see Derek smirking at us. He had won. He knew it. We knew it. And we hated him, with Dee and Leanne sharing looks of contempt with me about them.

This monitoring was how my music duties set me in the crossfire. Mark had occupied the music workstation, which was identical to all others except in two regards. First, it had the portable CD player, on which background music of Mark's choosing was always on (this was a CD we sold). Second, it had the CD rack of all albums we were selling. They rightly saw the desk as Mark's, but when he quit around the time that Karen and Derek were hired, that ceased to be true. And I became the heir-apparent to the music seat.

To write up my sales information for everyone, I requested access to Microsoft Word, but the custom order app we used resulted in a tightly controlled computer so that we could not access other programs. I was now a lone exception. Software licensing requirements meant it was easier to just install this on one workstation and have that be my regular, if not entirely official, seat. And the music spot was the obvious choice. Not only did this not stop Karen from repeatedly sniping that it belonged to her and trying to take it, but it seemed to inspire her to do so. Fortunately, all I had to do was say, "Jane," and our manager would make Karen get the fuck out. Of course, this made me Karen's enemy even more. The only real question was who the CSRs hated the most—Karen or Derek.

Ellen and I talked several times about the music work I was doing. I was unused to speaking with a company COO, but I have never been easily impressed and soon found myself on somewhat equal footing in the sense that I sometimes won an argument with her as she reluctantly conceded I had a point. I felt I was regaining some respect, but maybe I was just clueless.

I was volunteering to do these things, which meant they paid me no more for the extra work, which at first wasn't that bad. But as the months wore on, Ellen started ordering more and more CDs so that it became more time-consuming for me. And yet I was the only one required to listen to them and write sales information. Despite me having more work to do, others began acting like they were working hard entering mail orders and I was just kicking back with my feet up, checking out some tunes.

They also grew annoyed when, instead of allowing a piece of music play all the way, I skipped from one selection to the next, then skipped that after a minute. I didn't need to hear the whole thing to understand it all and write up what other products we had to upsell it with. They acted like I was ruining their enjoyment of something. While that was what the CD player had originally been for, it was now serving another purpose, and a business one. Even Jane sometimes gave me shit when I skipped ahead, while pressuring me to get on with it as fast as possible. They wanted to just enjoy the music instead of letting me do my additional job duties.

So much sniping came my way that I regretted ever doing any of it. This was true enough that, by summer, I told Jane I didn't want to do it anymore. It was making my coworkers resent me. I heard only negative remarks about it, as if I was the room's great slacker (that would be Derek). The additional work I had to do ironically had me seen as someone who was doing less work. Even a few of my best friends there gave me crap. And yet, when I gave my presentations about the music, which only I had to do, everyone thanked me profusely. Jane told me it was too bad and I couldn't stop. It was part of my job now. My volunteering had become mandatory.

By now, the monitoring of other CSRs had escalated, Dee and Leanne among the most vocal to me about it, always under their breath so Jane would not overhear. A few others in the room routinely frowned at Derek and Karen, seldom talking to them unless they needed to. Jane had taken to turning to look directly at me, and only me, when the phone rang. She didn't do it every time, but she didn't have to to get her point across. They considered me a poor employee, one who did less work. And I resented it.

In one particular incident, most of us had finished our batch of 50 mail orders, including me. This meant I had done just as much work as the rest of them. They were now free to do nothing if the phone didn't ring, but I was still reviewing and writing up CDs, working while they hung out. Seeing a remaining batch of mail orders, Karen stomped over to it, picked it up, and walked over to my desk, throwing it down so that it bounced off the surface and into my lap, then onto the floor.

"Get to work!" she snapped before going back to her desk.

I flushed with anger, especially as Derek began laughing across the room. This was far beyond inappropriate. I picked it up off the floor and rose, simmering as I walked toward our manager.

"Jane," I began, my voice cold, "Karen just picked up this stack of mail orders and threw it at me, demanding I enter them. You likely heard her do it. Half this room certainly did."

Jane turned around, looking a little uncomfortable and for once, stern, but she wore the disapproving look as if it didn't fit her. "Karen, this is not appropriate. We do not assign work to other people in this room."

"He's just sitting there listening to music!" Karen accused, defending herself. She said this like no one else in the room could hear the CD player.

Jane said, "He is reviewing those for everyone in this department to use. You are doing nothing right now, so you are going to enter these. And I don't want to see that again." She looked around the room. "That goes for all of you."

Jane's support surprised me. Karen met my hate-filled glare with her own. I dropped the mail orders in the basket she had taken them from and walked away. She stomped over to them and snatched them up before stomping back to her desk. Most of those in the room were women, and the roller skating one that was one of my best friends came over to talk to me quietly to see if I was okay, because I was fucking pissed and anyone could see it. I was pretty well liked at that job despite some digs at me, and no one liked Karen or Derek by now. The staff could almost have been divided into three groups: those who knew I was doing more than anyone and just as good a quality, those who stayed out of it, and those who thought I was a useless slacker, a group comprising Jane, Derek, and Karen.

With the tension mounting, Jane made it worse one day. Most of our orders came from individuals, but we often received an order from a library. These had to be entered a unique way that I never learned because no one would show me. I had repeatedly asked about it because these library orders came in the mail and I would sometimes end up with one and be unable to enter it, having been warned that special requirements existed. These orders were typically far larger than the usual 1-3 books, sometimes being over two dozen, so they took longer to do. Naturally, no one wanted the extra work. Despite my request to be shown how, I was not.

One day, it came up again, and when I asked Jane how to do it, she responded, "Just do it!"

"I don't know how."

"Stop being lazy!" she snapped.

I flushed in my chair, memories roaring back into focus. I am Learning Disabled, and in grade school, no one had known it. I'd had trouble with many of my assignments, but my teachers refused to believe I was trying. Instead, they had decided I was a troublemaker, and rather than helping, had resorted to punishing me. One of the most frequently made scathing comments, made before the entire class, was, "Stop being lazy!" I had heard it so many times that I could've been rich by the time I was twelve if I'd had a dollar for each time.

Some say that time heals all wounds, though I don't agree. After all, it doesn't exactly explain suicide. But sometimes the memory of trauma fades with the years. I had forgotten the awful emotions inherent in my struggles, the desperately deep feelings of inadequacy, the scorn, the vilification, the rejection of myself as a good kid trying my hardest but it being replaced by a false identity, that I was a jerk who deserved scorn and humiliation. But Jane said the same words my teachers had so often hurled at me with the same scorn that the memories roared into focus.

The color likely drained from my face. A crushing weight squeezed my heart.

Oh my God, I thought, in muted shock. *I forgot*. Sudden sympathy for the little boy I had once been filled me, the dark mindset and roiling emotions vivid and stunning. I tried to shake it off, but the next day, as I climbed the stairs to start my day there, my breathing became heavy, as if I were winded. I thought it would pass, and I went to an empty desk. Instead of logging in, I sat silently, still breathing heavy, no one else noticing me. It was getting worse, not better. I felt dazed, in a haze, as if disconnected from my body. I kept thinking to ask for help, but I felt too weak to speak. Something was happening to me. No one was looking at me. My distress rose. I felt afraid. And alone. I needed help. But no one saw.

Why isn't anyone looking at me?

I finally forced myself to my feet, grabbing onto the cube partition for support. My legs felt wooden. I stumbled forward, each step an effort. I touched each cube as I passed it in case I fell, but I made it past all of them toward the door. I opened it with an effort, because it felt heavy, like my legs. I stepped into the hall, and went directly into the HR room just beyond, where Ashley looked up at me, her curiosity turning to instant alarm.

"Oh my God," she said, jumping up. "You're as white as a sheet." She hurried around to me and took my arm just as I almost fell into one chair, legs giving way. "Are you okay?"

I shook my head, trying to speak and finding my tongue not cooperating.

"Do you want me to call an ambulance?"

The thought gave sudden weight to my symptoms, sobering me. What was happening to me? I nodded, confused and feeling vulnerable in the "I want my mommy" sort of way. I felt lost. Dizzy. Disoriented. Helpless. At the mercy of others.

I listened as she yelled for Jane and then called 911, my manager arriving to overhear the call as she sat down next to me and tried to help. I put one hand on my heart, which was pounding and felt like it was skipping beats horribly, adding a disjointed feeling that was both physical and mental. My breathing was still hard but slowed, which helped when one of them gave me a soda, my hand shaking as I tried to get it to my mouth, like it was too heavy for me. But when the liquid touched my tongue, the sugar was like a blast of clarity into my head and I gulped it down, draining half the can.

"Your color is returning," Ashely remarked.

That didn't surprise me. My breathing also slowed. "Thank you for this," I said, meaning the coke can. I felt much better.

"What happened?" Jane asked.

"I don't know."

Ashley said, "Well, the paramedics should be here in a minute."

And they were, and Ellen dropped by to see what was happening. By the time the ambulance had arrived, I had returned to normal and there was nothing for their instruments to detect. The EMTs said stress had caused a severe muscle spasm in my chest wall, directly over my heart, which had been impacted, causing my symptoms. They suggested that I just go home, so they called my parents, who picked me up. In retrospect, the hostile work environment triggered the attack.

By now, I had become known for my speed of data entry. Sometimes we received an extra batch of orders far over the usual, and for reasons I don't recall, they asked one person to enter the conference room and enter them instead of having to answer phones, too. I volunteered and set a new speed record, so it became another task mostly given to me. I wondered if it caused more resentment and envy or if anyone appreciated it. After all, while I was working my ass off, they had to take my share of the phone calls. It seemed like no amount of good would get me respected, just sniped at. It was like I worked only with "glass half empty" people.

One day I needed to continue my review of a massive box set of 25 Mozart CDs, but I couldn't find it in the CSR room. This was odd considering all of it was typically at the music workstation, which was where I was sitting, and no one knew anything else about the CDs, nor did they like classical music much.

"Has anyone seen the Mozart box set?" I asked.

Jane turned around. "I think I saw it in Ellen's office."

I smiled, and the way she smiled back, I knew we were thinking the same thing about going into the lion's den. "Soooo," I drawled, "would it be okay to go in there and get it?"

Her grin broadened. "*I'm* not going in there, but *you* can. Just be very polite and very careful and only admit I said it was okay if you have to."

I laughed as I got up. "If I don't return," I said to the room, "it was nice knowing all of you. Remember me fond-ly."

Figure 1 The Mozart Box Set

"Good luck!"

"Rest in peace!"

"We'll miss you, Rand!"

I was still laughing as I exited and went down the hall, reaching the rarely seen front desk. Sometimes the owners had business visitors, the receptionist greeting them there, but today she was absent and Sam sat there instead.

She had been there for years and worked in every department, so now she was a kind of freelancer working wherever needed, which was seldom in our room. She was a tall, butch lesbian who moved and spoke aggressively, with a "move the fuck over" vibe like some guys have. She referred to herself as a dyke and was quick to show you her unshaved legs by pulling up her corduroy trousers. Naturally, she didn't wear make-up or do a thing with her short brown hair, cut like a boy's. Her clothes were as brown and as unflattering as her mostly humorless demeanor, but this was a ruse. She didn't want to be your friend, didn't give a shit about anything, and wanted you to go away and not try to be chummy with her, so she acted standoffish on purpose. She refused to give me the time of day until my matter-of-fact remarks made her slowly realize I was a kindred spirit in not suffering fools gladly and being a wise-ass. Even then, she was only grudgingly accepting of me and sometimes favored me with a snarky comment just for me. I liked her and wondered how good she would be beside me in a bar fight.

Seeing me approach, she glanced at me and smirked before turning back to the computer before her. "What the fuck are *you* doing up here?"

I teased, "Hey Babe. I need to get something from Ellen's office."

She snorted in amusement. "Like hell you do."

"I'm serious. Is she in?"

"No. You want to get killed?"

"By you or her? Seriously, Jane approved it."

She laughed. "Are you sure she likes you?"

I joked, "Everyone does."

"Keep telling yourself that."

"Thanks. I will. Now if you'll excuse me."

I entered Ellen's small office, which I had been in a few times before, always to talk about the music stuff, always summoned by Her Majesty. My eyes searched the cluttered desk, chairs, and desks, but I saw no sign of the box, even after I went further in. Giving up, I turned around to exit and saw it sitting on top of a bookcase against the door's wall. It had been pushed up against a picture on the wall. I lifted it up and made my way from the room, but I had hardly taken two steps toward Sam when a crash and tinkling of glass sounded behind me. I stopped in disbelieving shock. Sam turned toward me, eyes wide, face sober. And then a muted smile seemed to appear in them, possibly from seeing my horrified expression.

"What the fuck did you do?"

As she got up and strode toward me, I slowly went back into Ellen's office, where she joined me in the doorway. Broken glass lay on the carpet, a shattered picture frame to one side. I stepped further in and looked at the place the CD set had been. The picture that had been against the wall was now on the floor. Apparently, it had not been hanging on a hook, but had been standing atop the bookcase. Ellen had held it up against the wall by placing the heavy box set against it, and when I took it, the picture fell forward and off, crashing into a chair and shattering. I said as much to Sam.

"Partly Ellen's own fault," she concluded, amused, "but you never heard me say that, and don't you dare repeat it."

"Yeah. Guess I better clean this up before she gets back."

"I'll do it. I suggest you get the fuck out of here. Go tell Jane."

I sighed, wondering if being fired was up next, but I didn't really think so. "Thanks," I muttered, walking away.

Jane looked suitably alarmed and went to see the damage, and eventually Her Majesty summoned me for my execution. But she pardoned me. That surprised me less than her look of acceptance that I would have naturally expected the picture to have been hanging on the wall and could not have known that would happen. Not known for her reasonableness, she was oddly polite in suggesting I always ask someone else to get it for me from now on. She didn't even make me pay for it when I offered to. But they enforced the policy about none of us setting foot outside the CSR room enforced with Draconian ruthlessness going forward. Everyone knew why, most of them amused by the story and telling me I only had eight lives left. I got the impression my popularity had risen. I was "the boy who lived," to quote Harry Potter.

It was around this time that I did something nice for Sam without her knowing it. She walked into the CSR room one day, irate that someone had stolen her six-pack of Coke cans from the break room fridge, saying she didn't care who did it, to just return them. No one fessed up, a few of us looking at each other in surprise at Sam's accusations. I suspected Derek had done it, as he seemed the type, but as I was in the break room later, I had an idea and set it in motion. I went to the soda machine and bought the number of missing Coke's while no one was looking, then went back into the break room and put them with her remaining ones. I was in a hurry because I didn't want anyone catching me doing it and thinking that I was the thief. A bit later, Sam returned to the CSR room, visibly surprised as she remarked that the thief had returned it all. I smiled to myself.

As the summer continued, I decided it was time to return to college. I hoped to earn a master's degree and then a PhD in music theory to become a college professor somewhere, hopefully also having my classical music sometimes performed. But I was aware that I might have to audition on classical guitar when I wasn't really interested in pursuing that. Just in case, I began practicing anyway, but a month later, the first signs of trouble appeared.

I had originally been a music composition major before transferring from a community college to Catholic University in D.C., not because I was Catholic (I wasn't), but because they had a good music department. And all other colleges I'd applied to had rejected me. It's a long story discussed in another memoir, *A Blast of Light*, but they forced me to change majors to classical guitar. While I was a guitarist, my genres for that were hard rock/metal and acoustic guitar music, not classical. I ended up agreeing to the change and needed to gain four years of classical guitar skill in the remaining two years. By heavily practicing, I succeeded, passing all performance tests to graduate. Then I put the classical guitar away, hadn't seen it since, and took the job at Icarus Books.

In August, a month into resuming my playing, my right arm grew tight and remained that way. It had been happening since the spring, but only for ten minutes at a time. This time, it didn't go away, and I was only using my left arm at work, mostly. But within a week, the left arm did it, too. I told work about it, sometimes taking a day off, and they seemed concerned at my obvious and constant pain. I finally went to a doctor, who diagnosed me with acute tendonitis in both arms. He administered a cortisone shot to both arms, but that only made me feel worse. I was increasingly concerned about my arms, because my best friend from college had gotten the injury, too, and it had taken a steep toll on his new career as a percussionist. My doctor gave me a note for reduced hours, and my job accommodated this, dropping me from six hours a day to five, but it didn't help.

As this was happening, Derek showed a lot of sympathy, to my surprise, asking me every day how my arms were doing and if I needed help with my mail orders, which Jane made others help me with, but it didn't improve things. Derek wanted to know what I couldn't do anymore, which was just about everything. Karen, being the bitch that she was, openly accused me of just trying to get out of doing more work, prompting Leanna to tell her to shut the fuck up in front of everyone, even Jane, who looked startled but didn't rebuke her for the language or anything else.

At my next doctor's appointment, he gave me a note recommending two weeks off, so I took them, hoping for relief. But it didn't come. My arms showed minimal improvement and when I returned to work, I had another note saying I couldn't handle the data entry work and that I needed other job duties.

"So you're quitting," Ashley stated, seeming anxious.

The question startled me. "Well, I was hoping there was something else I could do."

"There isn't. You're quitting?"

I wasn't sure if she seemed to resent it or what the subtle attitude about her came from. I felt like I was being pressured to quit and wasn't sure how to handle the situation. I said, "I don't know. I guess."

She suddenly seemed relieved. "Okay."

Ashley started getting paperwork for me to sign and within an hour, I had been unceremoniously shown the door, barely given a chance to say goodbye to my coworkers. Some of them were visibly surprised I had quit, since I hadn't told them I was going to. After all, I hadn't known it myself.

Before leaving, I exchanged phone numbers with Dee, a tall, thin black girl who had been one of my best friends there. We hung out once every week or two, usually going to see a movie. We weren't dating, just being friends, but her other friends and her mother kept teasing her that we were dating, and she eventually decided not being teased about that was more important than I was, so she refused to hang out anymore and I never saw her again. But before this, she had a surprise for me.

As we were driving somewhere, Dee said, "So there's something I've wanted to tell you but wasn't sure you wanted to know."

"Of course, now I want to know."

She laughed. "Yeah, but just hear me out before you say anything."

Wondering where this was going, I just said, "Okay."

"You remember when Derek was asking you all those questions about how your arms were doing, and what you couldn't do?"

"Yeah."

"Well, when you weren't there, he was making fun of you. He thought it was funny that you couldn't do all the things you like to do."

I flushed, feeling like a fool for having believed his concern was genuine. I should have known better. He was always an asshole. I didn't respond out loud and Dee continued.

"Also, and this part really makes me mad, but they made him full-time while you were gone those two weeks. They did it behind your back and everyone was told not to tell you."

I stiffened. A knife had been stuck in my back, and I hadn't even known. And it was a conspiracy, literally, to keep me from knowing about it, one that even my supposed friends, like Dee, had taken part in. And after they denied me full-time for so long, they skipped me for promotion for that asshole, of all people, and after all I had done with the music work. It was an incredible slap in the face, and to know that they had rewarded him with the promotion after he mocked my injury betrayed just about every idea I had about fairness. The girl who had been in line for full-time ahead of me had resigned over the tense working environment, meaning I had been next up if it ever happened.

By denying me full-time, they also denied me health care, and both short-term and long-term disability insurance, both of which I desperately needed because I was now severely disabled. But you can't get it when the injury has already taken place. They screwed me over great. I also wondered if their false accusation that I had tried to get myself full-time earlier that year had led them to skip me in retaliation. I had gone from being praised for finding the error in the 2000 CDs to being treated like shit.

"I wasn't going to tell you all of this," Dee continued, and I wondered why she was telling me now, "but something else just happened. He was just diagnosed with carpal tunnel syndrome in one hand and can't use it anymore."

Despite my anger, I laughed. Dee heard it and started, too. "That's awesome."

"Yeah, this is why I'm telling you. I knew you would love that."

"Thank you. So they fired him?"

She sighed. "No. That's the other thing that pisses me off. He came in with a doctor's note saying he needed light duties and they gave it to him."

"What?" I asked in disbelief. I had asked for the same thing and had been shown the door.

"He's working in Fulfillment now, pulling books. This is so unfair. Everyone knows it, too, after what they did to you, so people are really mad now. I mean, people hate Jane, Ashley, and Ellen. Well, people always hated Ellen. They keep talking about quitting. We hate Derek and won't even say hello to him."

I felt a little relief on hearing this. Not everyone was a backstabbing asshole. Dee mentioned names to me and said people kept asking her for updates on how I was doing, even people who hadn't been friendly toward me, like Sam. It was nice to know some of them cared, and in my dreams, they would have quit en masse to protest, but I knew they wouldn't and didn't blame them. Still, that management had made all their staff disrespect them felt good. They deserved it. They didn't seem to know the value I had brought, or that I was a decent guy and Derek and Karen were the two assholes, but it said a lot about them that they rewarded him for his behavior and showed me nothing but contempt for mine. They deserved each other.

But the whole thing rankled. I had been discarded, just like the remaindered books and CDs they sold for profit. My life had imploded, leaving me severely disabled and unable to do much of anything, my future shattered and gone. All that remained of my life was watching TV or reading a book. I had fully descended into the hell that is recounted in a major memoir, *The Wine-Dark Sea*.

In the years that followed, Icarus Books added "and Music" to their company name as they branched out into a full music division. Before my involvement, they only included a few CDs in their book catalog. By the time of my departure, I had written many music guides for sales staff, I was the sole person reviewing all the music and writing sales materials for them and doing presentations, and I had instigated a separate music catalog that hadn't come to fruition yet. I do take credit for raising Ellen's seriousness about that area of the business. Who knows what could have happened if they had treated me with any decency instead of kicking me to the curb?

But I doubt I would have ended up some sort of executive of Icarus Books and Music. They showed their contempt for me while I worked there and capped it off during my departure, so rewarding me with a prominent role in the division I helped inspire probably would not have happened anyway. Eventually, the owners sold the business and retired so that nothing remains.

Karma Delivered

The belief that doing a good job at work will lead to promotions, esteem, and other benefits is among the more foolish ones permeating society. Sure, it sounds cynical, and maybe it is. Or maybe it's just realistic. What is less deniable is that, without this idea, no one would do their job well and would do just enough to avoid getting fired. Even worse is the possibility that working hard might actually cost you your job.

I ran into this reality at my first job. Having just turned eighteen and graduated high school, I took a job at Parcel Fast loading packages into 18-wheelers. It was brutal work, so much so that you could only work a 4-hour shift. Some guys work a back brace, but I was healthy and had spent years working out at Gold's Gym, though I wasn't some buff Adonis—actually I was; I'm just trying to be modest. Sorry about that.

The job began with weeks over a dozen trainees learning how the operation worked and the roles in it. Outside the huge, gray, concrete warehouse, 18-wheelers backed up to it and left their trailers at one of the four exterior walls. Some were full of packages that needed unloading, the contents placed onto the conveyer belts that carried them through a maze of metal machinery, much of it on stilts to raise it far off the floor. Steel walkways and ladders allowed the people who worked as sorters to get up there and route the packages down chutes or onto other belts. All of it obstructed visibility despite the building being three stories high and one giant, open room with no upper floors, except maybe in a corner for offices. The place smelled of cardboard, grease, and sweat, and people had to yell to be heard over the noise of machines, or boxes sliding down metal chutes that sometimes buckled, flexed, and thundered from the weight on them.

While some packages were destined for loading into local delivery trucks, others were to be manually re-stacked in another big trailer, and this was my job. For this, they divided areas of the building into stations for eight trucks each, a manager overseeing the eight truck loaders. He reported to another guy who managed three stations, and there appeared to be three or four such guys, meaning twelve stations, with eight trucks. They all reported to the shift manager who ran the building, which was in operation 24/7.

As a truck loader, my job was to stand inside my trailer and deal with the packages that slid off the metal chute and into it. The two station sorters were the ones who sent them here. They stood facing each other, the belt in between, packages coming at them from one side. If I was a sorter, I grabbed a package and, depending on its zip code, shoved it down the chute two to my right, immediately on my right, just on my left, or two over on my left. Or I tossed it into the same setup of silver chutes across from me and beside the other sorter. This determined which of the eight trucks on the station the package went into, and it was also why there were only eight trailers on a station. For sorters, only minimal lifting was involved, and since they determined where packages went, they were paid more. And both were reasons I wanted to be promoted to one.

But I was a truck loader. My job was to stack the boxes coming into my truck. This isn't complicated, but big, heavy boxes don't go atop small, light ones or the contents will be crushed. Small, heavy boxes don't go on top of big, light ones for the same reason. Naturally, the deepest part of the trailer is filled first.

But first, I had to double-check the zip code, because sorters make mistakes and if the package goes to the wrong destination, which could be halfway across the country, this delays delivery and makes Parcel Fast look bad. They tracked these bad packages as a metric of how well people were doing. They told us our stats every day, in front of our coworkers on the station, to motivate each other by hearing who was doing well or bad. And the overall performance affected our manager, Charles, so he wanted us to know when we were making him look good. Or bad. And this was where my troubles began.

It started with Charles, a black man in his thirties. He wore a button up blue shirt and khakis, unlike his staff, as we wore athletic shorts and t-shirts for the sweat-inducing work. He managed the "orange" station where I worked in my after-dinner shift. His job seemed simple. If someone needed a bathroom break, he took over their truck, or switched with the sorter. He made sure no one got behind. He gave our team a pep talk before a shift and called out those who had an especially good or bad error rate for their truck.

After training, they assigned me to Charles' station and given one of the two worst trucks in the entire building, the Hunt Valley Maryland truck. The zip codes were the distinguishing trait. The five-digit codes all started with 210, 211, or 212. But it wasn't all of them. That would make three hundred numbers, but if it was everything from 21000 to 21299, that would have essentially been three numbers: anything starting with 210, 211, or 212. Instead, there were only about 100 zip codes out of those 300, and they were utterly random. They gave me a sheet of paper with 100 numbers to memorize. Some other guy on my station had a truck with one zip code. One. Most had ten to twenty, but there was another poor schlep like me—my truck was on the far end of our station, and his was on the opposite side and also had 210, 211, and 212 zip codes, but about forty of them. Someone was evil to do this.

Making this worse for me was that I was born Learning Disabled. My experiences with this are recounted in another memoir, *Refusal to Engage*, but I have trouble learning random information or anything that is told to me verbally. Since I had a list of numbers taped to the truck, or in my pocket at all times, this was less of an issue, but being Learning Disabled also made me pretty bad with numbers, especially random ones devoid of meaning. I asked for a different truck due to my concerns, not admitting to the reason because I don't like being treated differently over being Learning Disabled, or using it as an excuse, but they refused.

Not surprisingly, Charles gave me and the other guy a lot of help at first. Like the sorters, he had to know all eight trucks on his station. But we were soon on our own. My peers found my predicament amusing at first, and sometimes they tried to help but failed. They would get a 210-212 package in their truck because a sorter screwed up, and when this happened to any of us, we were supposed to place it outside our own truck. When we had a moment (because the flow of packages had slowed), we brought it to the right truck on our station; sometimes it didn't belong on any of them, and Charles took them away. Otherwise, we put these boxes inside the right truck and the loader there double-checked it and stacked it. But many times guys brought me a 210XX-212XX package, and I told them it was not mine. They would argue and refuse to take it away. And so the attitudes started.

And they got worse. At first, I had my fair share of bad packages that had gotten past me and loaded, but my error rate plummeted, and Charles repeatedly singled me out in our pre-shift meetings. I felt pleased and initially got the "good job" stuff from peers, but the more Charles praised me, the less I heard that and the more I heard grumblings from my coworkers. At the time I didn't care about the jealousy, wrongly thinking it would not matter.

I distinguished myself in another way. Sometimes a truck got slammed. This meant that an unusual volume of packages headed for a single truck in a short period (now!) and a single person could not keep up with the flow. The packages would clog the chute, falling off it, and creating a pile inside the truck, one that you could hardly navigate. A station manager sometimes helped with this, or another guy on that station (and ofttimes several people), but sometimes a call went out to the entire building for a volunteer. And somehow, I became the go-to guy for the full building. Other people did it, too, of course, but I sometimes did it two or three times a night.

And one reason was that I needed the mental break. My truck's zip codes were rough, and when I went to help someone else, they checked the packages for their truck, and I got ten minutes to just stack boxes and not think about them. But I was also trying to do well, and it was working. Charles worked for Robbie, who oversaw three stations and their managers, and Robbie stopped by to first meet me, then to find out what my ambitions (be a sorter), and then increasingly, he was the one who ran to our station and specifically grabbed me as we ran off to help someone else. If the station was his, he always asked for me. If it was another station run by another team, he still came to get me because he could earn points with other managers at his level, the same way that I was doing.

For a while there, it seemed like the myth of doing a good job and being rewarded was working. While I didn't get a raise, Charles and Robbie both valued me. I started asking about becoming a sorter. I was told to keep my bad package numbers low and they would see about it. But then the trouble started.

While I was helping someone who was getting slammed, I was obviously not at my truck. Charles needed to take care of it for me, which was a major reason he had to approve of a request for me to leave for 5-15 minutes. Once I was the go-to guy, I never made the requests to go; he either offered me (without asking me because he knew I would say yes) or Robbie was asking him (and he couldn't tell his manager "no"). I would just get a shout from one of them that I was off to whatever color station it was. I always knew why. There was only one reason. I initially had to be escorted through the labyrinthian maze of metal to reach another station, but I soon knew where all of them were.

Sometimes I returned to my truck to find packages everywhere, even clogging the chute because no more could fit into the mess inside. No one had been taking care of my truck. There I had been, helping someone else, and neither my manager nor my team had my back. Charles even swung by and gave me shit about it sometimes.

"Come on, Rand," he said, walking by on the metal grate that ran along the wall, a few feet down from the truck's rear, "clean that shit up."

Indignant, I said, "I just got back and found it like this."

"Well, clean it up."

Trying to not give an attitude, I said, "You know if you're gonna volunteer me to help other people, you can at

least keep my truck in decent shape while I'm doing it."
While I tended to mumble at that age, so much noise surrounded me that I practically had to shout to be heard and so my speech issues seldom arose.

He smiled because he knew I was right. "Yeah, alright, man. Next time."

And sometimes he did. But he often didn't, and I started to expect a mess when I got back, and some of the other truck loaders on my belt would stand around doing nothing instead of helping.

At one of our pre-shift meetings, Charles said, "Rand, for the last couple days, you had three times as many bad packages in your truck as anyone else on this station. You need to shape up if you want to be a sorter. That's not gonna cut it."

Shock. Going from one of the best hardly seemed possible. "Are you serious?"

Several coworkers beside me snickered, and he said, "Yeah. Come on man, I know you can do better."

I walked away to start my shift, irritated. I made sure nothing bad got into my truck, but it happened again. And again. I didn't understand it. There was no way I was loading bad packages. I had started in June and it was now late summer. I had that Hunt Valley truck memorized and never looked at my list of zip codes anymore. Until now. I began reviewing it, but I knew it all. I even knew the other 210XX-212XX truck because I'd worked it a few times when the usual guy was out and no one else but Charles could (or the sorters, who weren't coming down to do it, the snobs that they were).

And then I realized the obvious reason for the spike in my error rate—while I helped other people who were getting slammed, Charles sometimes made my coworkers load my truck instead of doing it himself. And they were putting the bad packages in there, whether on purpose, by accident, or through the indifference they regularly showed. It explained the snickers every time Charles had said something in front of me. It explained them arguing about a package not going in my truck, sometimes throwing it in even after I told them it didn't belong there. My coworkers either didn't care or were sabotaging my truck. So much for teamwork.

Shortly after I figured this out, I asked Charles if I could talk to him and he refused. Was he concerned the others would see us talking about something? But later he stuck his head in my trailer and told me to report to another slammed truck. I told him I wasn't going unless I could talk to him first, so he went with me to talk along the way. This was usually at a brisk jog, but we walked this time.

I asked, "Are you watching my truck while I'm gone, or is someone else doing it?"

"Usually someone else."

We walked around a stack of pallets. "Yeah, I thought so. Look, they're the ones putting the bad packages in my truck."

"Come on, man, they wouldn't do that."

"I'm not saying they're doing it on purpose, but we both know no one else can handle my truck, just you and me. Think about it."

He seemed to realize I was right, so I felt relieved, but he also seemed like he wouldn't admit it. Was it because it was ultimately his fault, not mine? He was technically responsible for my truck in my absence and had been pawning it off on someone else, and I was paying the consequences (along with people whose packages were significantly delayed), but if the truth came out, he would look bad. But I wasn't interested in blaming him. I just wanted it to stop.

As we walked between the metal stilts holding up another conveyer belt above, I said, "Can you just take care of it for me instead of letting one of them do it?"

"Yeah, man, sure." He sounded dismissive and completely unconvincing.

"Because if it keeps happening, I'm not doing these slammed trucks anymore."

"We need you to."

"And I need to know you have my back." I was trying not to point out that I was doing him and others a favor that benefitted them, but was now costing me—because of him. I resented what he was doing and his less than stellar response. I couldn't help airing another grievance. "I keep coming back to find my truck a mess, too. This was supposed to be a deal. I help and make both of us and Robbie look good. You keep my truck in line while I'm doing it." I stopped there, sensing I was going to give my manager too much shit.

"All right, man, I'll take care of it."

I didn't believe him, but there wasn't much else I could say other than a matching, half-assed, "Thanks."

Despite all of this, they allowed me to try sorting on a couple slow nights, for only an hour. The guy across from me was condescending about me becoming a sorter on the hardest station (because of the two 210XX through 212XX trucks I already knew), making snide remarks that I wouldn't be able to handle it. He acted like he was so far above me on the food chain, but then he was young and stupid like me.

The error rate in my truck rose and fell, and while I wasn't writing down the nights that I went to help slammed trucks, and the resulting spike in my error rates reported a day or two later, I knew they correlated. Charles wasn't pulling his weight, and I began asking who had taken care of my truck in my absence, implying that it was so that I could say thanks. And I did, but I asked people to please verify the packages. This was likely seen as telling people how to do their job when they already knew, which was true, but what else could I do? It was met with coworkers making snide remarks that I apparently was not so much better at this than them after all. Or they gave me the finger, or told me to go fuck myself. If another of them overheard this, that person would laugh to support that response.

And this was how I knew they were loading bad packages into my truck on purpose, to put me in my place. The rate of it rose out of their spite, which was why Charles and Robbie called me into a pre-shift meeting in October. The office was tiny, barely enough for a small desk and two chairs, the one Robbie sat in and mine across from him, Charles leaning against the wall.

"Rand," said Robbie, a short, white, athletic preppy with curly blonde hair, "your error rate is unacceptable. You are the worst one in the entire building now."

I was angry at having this distinction. I also felt embarrassed and defensive. Scowling, I said, "I am not the one doing this."

He cut me off. "The truck is your responsibility."

I thought he was going to say more and jumped in. "Not when I'm away helping slammed trucks. Then the truck is Charles' responsibility."

"That's true. Don't you think he knows that truck better than you?"

Actually, no, I did not think that, but he certainly knew it just as well. But that wasn't the point. "It doesn't matter if he's not the one working it while I'm gone."

Robbie looked surprised and turned to Charles with a raised eyebrow.

Looking uncomfortable, Charles admitted, "Sometimes I can't be watching it and someone else is helping."

Like he understood what was going on, Robbie observed politely, "They don't really know that truck though, I'm guessing."

Having a chip on my shoulder, I said with an attitude, "They don't care either. They tell me off if I ask them to set aside any package that they aren't sure about. They think it's funny that my error rate went up. They're doing it on purpose."

Robbie held up a hand. "Well, let's not go too far. That's a pretty serious thing to say."

"It's true. Ask Charles. They laugh about it. To my face."

Robbie again turned to Charles, who again looked uncomfortable, which was itself an admission that I was telling the truth. Robbie sighed. "Okay, I get it. I'm sorry. This is partly on me. We'll get this straightened out. Please keep ensuring only the right packages are loaded. Have a good shift."

I got up and left by myself, feeling like Robbie was on my side and still reasonable. Had I acquitted myself well? I didn't have long to wonder, because Charles caught up to me and as he fell in beside me said, "That wasn't good, Rand."

That surprised me, but I didn't care. I was pissed at him now and didn't respond. He had gotten me in trouble with his manager, the dick. I didn't realize at the time that I had just thrown him under the bus to *his* manager and likely had a target on my back now, not that it would have mattered. He was screwing me over anyway. How much worse could he do?

At first, the situation cleared up a bit, but not enough, and within weeks, I was once again called into a meeting. This time it was Robbie and his manager Sam, the guy who ran the entire building for the night shift. Sam was in his 50s, balding, congenial, and in the same button-up shirt and khakis as all the managers. He sat across from me behind his desk, with what turned out to be an open folder with data about me in it in front of him. Robbie stood off to one side, legs spread, hands clasped behind him. A couple other people stood behind me as I sat in the hard metal inquisition chair. Before anyone opened their mouth, I knew what was going on and half expected to be fired.

"Listen Randy," began Sam, his tone conciliatory, and my strong impression was that he was a good guy, "I'm concerned about what's happening with your error rate, and I don't understand it. I'd like to know what's going on. You were the one of most promising people and now have the worst rate. I have to be frank with you. Normally we would have just fired you by now."

A jolt of adrenaline tore through me. That f-bomb wasn't one to say lightly. I was on the verge of being fired right now, depending on what I said. And it was my first job! I felt insecure, alarmed, and angry at the reason for all of it. It was like I was being framed by my asshole coworkers and managers.

Sam flipped through the papers. "I understand you want to be a sorter, but with error rates like these, there's no way I can promote you. I've also known for months now that you've built quite an excellent reputation for helping any truck getting slammed. This is one reason you're still employed. Can you tell me what's going on?"

I almost laughed. "Yeah, me helping those other trucks is exactly what's going on." And so I told him the truth, defending myself and trying to save my job.

"Does Charles know about this?"

I scowled in disbelief. "Yeah, of course he does. So does he!" I pointed my accusing finger at Robbie. "They both said they would make sure it stopped happening, but nothing has changed. I said repeatedly that I don't want to help any more slammed trucks because of this, but they both refuse to let me stop. It was supposed to be voluntary, but now they expect it and won't let me say no, like it's part of my job. And now it's going to cost me my job. And there's nothing I can do about it!"

Sam turned to look at a visibly uncomfortable Robbie, and I could tell from Sam's demeanor that he believed me. Being indignant has its advantages. Sadly, it also had its downfalls, like throwing your manager's manager under the bus to *his* manager. In retrospect, it makes me laugh, but I was just mad.

Sam asked Robbie, like he already knew the answer, "Is this all true?"

Robbie hesitated. Could he tell I was a reliable witness in my defense? Was there a written report from our previous meetings that would back up my claims? If so, it seemed that Sam hadn't seen it, but then maybe it was in my personnel file and he didn't have access to that. I didn't know how that sort of thing worked, and I also wondered if the reports of those meetings were accurate or full of bullshit meant to protect someone's ass other than mine. I was suspicious and felt like I was the only honest person in this situation, with the possible exception of Sam.

"Well," began Robbie, "we've been aware that others can't really handle the truck, and we've had no choice but to have them loading it when Charles just couldn't take over."

Wryly, Sam observed, "Well, if Charles can't take over, then maybe we shouldn't be volunteering Randy at those times."

Robbie nodded. "Yeah, we can make sure that doesn't happen from now on."

"Randy or Charles. No one else. I want you to make it clear to that team that no one loads something in that truck without one of them verifying it. We have to get this under control."

"Understood."

"Also, if Randy doesn't want to go, he doesn't have to. No more volunteering him."

"Yes, sir."

Sam turned to me. "We'll give this a shot and see how it goes. If no one else works that truck and the error rates drop, that's great. I really appreciate your honesty. I feel confident this will get resolved and we'll all go back to being happy."

I felt so relieved and loved this guy. "Great. *Thank* you. I really appreciate it."

"Sure. Thank you. Head over to your shift. Robbie, stay here a minute."

I felt great as I left. No more coworkers sabotaging me. No more resentment. No more Charles letting me down or setting me up to fail. Robbie, too. No more forced volunteering. No more threat of being fired. I would refuse to help a slammed truck for a week or two and show them I was right about all of this. The error rate would plunge, exonerating me. And people who needed help with their truck could kiss my ass because I had to look out for my own.

Being a clueless teenager, I had no awareness that I had just thrown Robbie under the bus to his manager, but it was his own damn fault. He silently stood there and listened as I got hauled under the bus, knowing it was the whole point of the meeting ahead of time. What did he think I was going to do? Take a bullet for him? What the hell was he doing for me? How did he think this worked? Was he expecting me to keep my mouth shut, that I wouldn't have the balls to do what I had just done? Balls really had nothing to do with. I was being falsely accused and would not sit there and take it. I'd rather be honest and deal with the consequences than accept blame for something I wasn't responsible for.

But my words to Sam may have explained what happened next.

Days later, I called in sick shortly before my shift. I had a fever, my nose was running, and my throat and lower back really hurt. I was in no condition to be doing physically demanding work, especially something so strenuous that Parcel Fast only let you do a four-hour shift. Shortly before I was supposed to start, my mother told me that my manager was on the phone. I reluctantly picked up, expecting Charles, but it was Robbie.

"We need you to come in."

"I can't. There's no way I can do that." I explained my symptoms and he wouldn't take no for an answer, repeatedly observing that they were short staffed because so many people had called in sick. He tried flattering me about how good I was, that no one could handle my truck. He even mentioned our mutual resolve to ensure no bad packages ended up in it, as if I had loyalty to the trailer when I only gave a shit about that truck when it was my job to load it. If I didn't show up, it wasn't my problem and an error report would be about someone else, not me. Or would it? Was it still as my truck even if I wasn't there and I would get blamed anyway? I felt irritated and frustrated, wanting to hang up on him. And I finally said something to appease him.

"Look, the only way I could come in is if I'm sorting."

"We could do that! We'll have you sort tonight."

Normally I would have been pleased because I had only been allowed to sort for under an hour before. This could be my chance, a full shift, but I still felt like shit and wanted to make sure he knew something. "I am not setting foot in my truck."

"Yeah, we'll have someone else take care of it. We really need you. I'll see you when you come in. Thanks, Randy!"

He hung up, and I frowned, feeling manipulated and having myself to blame. I shouldn't have offered that. Now I had to go in. I dragged myself upstairs to change my clothes and stuffed my pockets full of cough drops and tissues, taking another dose of liquid medicine and fever reducers as I left. It was only four hours of standing and shoving packages into chutes. Maybe I would survive.

As I walked into work through the open bay door at the building's corner, the familiar whir and clatter of metal machinery reached my ears. I was technically late, the shift already underway, but I got a free pass because I hadn't been planning to be there. Robbie happened to be approaching me at a jog as we both turned the corner toward my station and trailer.

"Hey, come on, a truck is getting slammed." He kept jogging.

I scowled. "I am not loading trucks tonight. Come on, man."

He called over one shoulder, "The truck is yours."

I swore. I walked faster but refused to run past the training station or the next one over. My orange station came into view and I saw two sorters above doing their thing. My truck was the farthest one and both Robbie and Charles were now inside, checking zip codes and stacking the boxes. I intended to only check the packages, not load them, but Robbie hopped out, saying he had to be somewhere.

"Take over," he said.

"I am *not* stacking boxes," I insisted.

"Just a minute until this is cleared up," he said. "Then we'll get you up to sorting."

I glared, but he walked away, leaving me with Charles, who said, "Come on."

I angrily climbed into the Hunt Valley truck and went for the lightest boxes, and within a few minutes, they were all cleared. Charles jumped out of the truck.

"Where are you going?" I asked in disbelief. "I'm not doing this."

"To see about getting you up to sorting. Hold on."

I couldn't argue with that, but my back was really bothering me now. I reluctantly stacked more boxes as they came in, taking my time, not worrying much about a mess accumulating because someone else would take it over and I wasn't doing this shit. The minutes ticked by as I grew surly, having to pull tissues from my pocket and wipe my nose, but having nowhere to put them after, so I threw them out onto the grate and kept working. Over the next ninety minutes, Charles repeatedly refused to send me up to sorting. I sometimes left my truck and went looking for him, only to be given another excuse and told not to leave my truck without permission. As this happened, my coworkers sometimes saw me and gave me the finger, which had become a thing. Maybe when I was sorting, I would send a shit ton of bad packages to their trucks and make them carry each to the right one, or hope they screwed up and loaded it anyway. They would have deserved it. Two could play that game.

My mood steadily descended into blackness as my body ached. I suspected this had all been a setup. Robbie had no intention of letting me sort. Neither did Charles. They were fucking with me, getting back at me for shining a light on how they were already screwing me over. Fuck them. My anger soared. Thoughts of quitting grew and grew as I fantasized about it between holding my sore throat or back in pain, or wiping my nose and throwing the tissue out on the metal grate, only to have Charles give me an attitude for it and yell at me to clean it up.

"Get me out of this truck!" I demanded.

"We're working on it."

Bullshit! I thought. I finally couldn't take it anymore and sat down on a box to rest, sweat dripping from me, my head feeling light. I just wanted to go home. Fuck sorting. Fuck them being understaffed. Fuck this truck. None of this was my problem. My asshole managers, obnoxious coworkers, and this stupid job were my problems. And I knew they would never let me sort. If even this wouldn't get me it, nothing would, and Robbie had promised but lied to me. I had contempt for them all.

One of my coworkers stepped up to my trailer and tossed a light but sizeable box at me, hitting my leg with it. "Get up, you lazy fuck! You are the most worthless piece of shit on this crew!"

"Fuck you!" I yelled, and he cackled as he walked away.

Sudden rage overtook me and I rose and jumped out of the truck onto the grate, then quickly went down the metal steps to the concrete floor, striding toward the exit. Charles saw me from a distance and tried to catch up with me, as I was steps from leaving the area of our station without permission and he likely knew something was up from my angry body language.

"Where are you going?"

"I fucking quit," I snapped over one shoulder, not stopping. Every word hurt my throat.

"What? Are you serious?"

"Why the hell would I not be serious? You won't get me out of that fucking truck, so I'm doing it myself."

"We'll get you up to sorting in five minutes."

"You've said that for the last hour and a half!" I yelled. For all my misery, anger had given me energy, and I easily kept ahead of him and would remain so unless he broke into a jog.

My sincerity seemed to get through to him and his tone changed to pleading as he continued trying to catch up. "Come on, man, don't quit."

"I already did," I snapped.

"You can't just walk out."

"Watch me."

"No, I mean you have to go to HR and do paperwork."

I hadn't thought of that. "Whatever."

"Do you know where it—"

"I know where it is," I said. "Go have fun loading my truck for the rest of your life."

He stopped following me and I never saw him again. I stomped right into the HR woman's office and announced I was quitting immediately. Visibly startled by my anger, she asked if I was sure or wanted to talk about it, but I wasn't in the mood for conversation. But when she offered to have me fill out a grievance report, cold cruelty took my heart, and I eagerly accepted it, sitting in an open room and writing at length about what had been happening. Everyone went under the bus and I repeatedly backed over them with wild wrath.

Robbie walked in at some point, and I shot him a cold glance that kept him from approaching me. He went to talk to the HR woman and left after a minute. When I handed my grievance report to her and she read it, she looked up at me in amazement.

"Are you sure you want to file this?"

"Absolutely."

I had little sense about not burning bridges and other such things at that age, but I still sensed that I would likely never work at Parcel Fast again once that was filed. I couldn't have cared less. It wasn't like I was coming back. I would never see these people again. Let them burn in a raging inferno of incorrectly sorted cardboard packages, stacked around them so that they couldn't get out, and the person best able to clear the mess was the one who had boxed them in and set it all ablaze.

The Stand Up

Being stood up is one of the least enjoyable results of dating, and we seldom learn the reason it happened. I was more fortunate with one experience, and the justification I was given had me wishing I could always discover the truth.

I met Lisa via a personal ad of hers in 2000, when online dating was considered weird, something only losers who still lived with their parents did. We met for a drink at a nearby bar to test our attraction and connection, which was strong enough for a second and third date. For each, I suggested somewhere in public such as a restaurant, and made arrangements, picked her up, and paid the tab, taking steps like making my car—and myself—presentable. She reciprocated, not looking as if she had just rolled out of bed, but like the date mattered enough for some polish, so I felt the mutual interest growing stronger.

Throughout, she laughed easily, seemed genuine, and showed an interest in my aspirations as a musician and author. While she expressed little ambition herself, she appealed to me for her willingness to explore life and see what possibilities unfolded. This struck me as the opposite of jaded, and I liked that. She responded warmly to my laid-back, joking style, while I found her direct gaze and no-nonsense approach refreshing. I had never been one for bullshit. Her earnestness helped keep me engaged when the first signs of trouble arose.

And the sign was that she proved remarkably difficult to reach, and I wondered if this told me something. But we ended up in bed together, so I was getting mixed signals about her interest. Unsure what to think, I continued trying in the hope that it would sort itself out. This was long before the smartphone, and only some of us owned a cellphone, with limited voice mail and sometimes no texting available. This meant leaving a message at someone's home or via email that they could only check at a computer. Neither explained the long delays before she would answer. For example, early in a week, I sometimes suggested a date for Friday and didn't even get a reply until Saturday. I was certain she was aware of these and just wasn't replying to my invitation, and yet when she finally called, she was friendly if dodging the issue. I didn't know how to interpret this and suspected she was playing games.

Despite this, we finally had a fourth date at my apartment, where I would cook breaded chicken, fettuccine, and steamed vegetables for us. Then we'd settle in for a rented movie I had picked up after we agreed on one. She was to arrive at 6:30, dinner by 7pm. I confirmed that afternoon that she was still coming, one of the rare times she actually picked up when I called, so I was doing my thing in the kitchen shortly after 6pm, having straightened up and doing the usual prep we all do, especially the first time a date is coming over.

But by 6:45, there was no sign of her. Or at 7pm, when I called and got her voice mail, leaving a message that dinner was ready and I hoped everything was okay. I checked my messages. Nothing. Was she standing me up? Or had something happened? How long was I supposed to have faith? If

I had been waiting in public, I might have already left to spare myself humiliation of being seen getting stood up. Since I was home, it was less obnoxious, but it's still unpleasant going through the mix of hope, trying to stay positive, and ignoring your gut, fighting the feeling of impending rejection.

You practice various responses. Anger? It shows you care, and yet guys are taught to act unfazed as a sign of strength. Indifferent? It allows someone to "walk all over you" and is weak. Concern that something has happened? It shows strength in that you are assuming she couldn't possibly be standing *you* up, but makes you sound like a fool to not realize that's exactly what she's doing. Indecision about these? Also lame.

By 7:30 she was an hour late and I called again, but I didn't leave a message, having not found a suitable way to express my unhappiness. At 8pm I tried again, hung up, and then warmed up the cold food, eating dinner alone, feeling stupid for not accepting sooner what was happening. And by 8:30 I called one last time, once again getting her voice mail. But this time I had my response worked out, and I tried to keep any upset out of my voice, and give her the benefit of the doubt, even though I knew better—it made me feel dumb doing it, but it's still better than saying something rude only to find out she's been in an accident and is in the hospital, for example.

"Hey Lisa, it's Randy. It's two hours after you were going to be here, so at least call and let me know you're okay." I paused, then couldn't help adding, "It's way past the point of looking like you stood me up."

Then I hung up and went about the rest of my night without her. She didn't call then or the next day, when I emailed asking if she was okay. I repeated this for several more days, during which I was increasingly sure she was fine and ghosting me long before I had heard the term. I finally left a message saying I wasn't going away until she answered me, even though that wasn't true, but being ignored is as awful as anything else in dating and I wanted a reply, regardless of what it was.

And I finally got one when the phone rang.

"Hello?"

"I did *not* stand you up."

That she couldn't be bothered to say hello first told me she was angry. So was I, the upset I had held back closer to the surface now that I sensed a hostile presence. But I wanted to be civil and settled for sarcasm, the respect I had felt for her mostly gone. "Ah, hi Lisa. Nice to hear you're okay. So what do you call it when you don't show up for a date or let me know you aren't coming?"

"I was busy."

A lovely answer. She might as well have said I wasn't important. I kinda knew that by now. Even so, it's not one of those things you're supposed to confirm. I could already tell she was never going to admit she'd stood me up. And now I felt only contempt and curiosity what she would say next. Relaxed amusement mixed with muted disapproval filled me. "Doing what? We had a date."

"My parents stopped by right before I was going to leave."

I paused, confirming, "That wasn't planned?"

"Of course not. We had a date."

"Okay, so you at least admit that we had one. Why didn't you tell them you had to go out?"

"I didn't want to be rude."

I scowled. "How is that rude? You had plans. If anything, them dropping by unannounced is rude."

"They're my parents."

That was apparently a cart blanche to do whatever they pleased. Was she unable to stand up to them? "Does that mean you can't tell them they're interrupting your plans and you're sorry but you have to go? Or at least call the person you have plans with to say that you're going to be late, or you're not going to make it at all?"

"I didn't want to be rude."

I frowned. "To who? How is it rude to tell them the truth? Don't you think they would feel bad if they found out you stood me up on account of them? My parents would never stop by unannounced because they understand I have a life and plans, and if they did it, I would say it was nice of them to drop by, but I have to go in a few minutes and next time they should call first."

"Well, I'm not as rude as you are."

I laughed in disbelief, pacing around in my apartment, the portable phone to one ear. "You're the one who stood me up, but I'm the one who is rude?"

"I did not stand you up."

"Did you hear the phone ringing? Because that was me, wondering where you were."

"Of course I heard it."

"And you didn't pick up."

"I was busy being gracious. You don't answer the phone when you have guests."

I laughed at her assessment of her conduct, but in a way she had a point. But there's a reason the phrase "excuse me" exists, and it's so you can be *gracious* to *everyone*. She acted as if being gracious to her parents gave her free rein to be rude to anyone else. She seemed remarkably deferential to them, and equally unable to acknowledge that the result was rudeness to me. I said as much, and she changed the subject.

"I was going to call you back after they left."

"But you didn't," I observed.

"Because when I listened to the voice mail, I was mad that you thought I was standing you up."

Disbelief struck me hard. "It was two hours later! How long am I supposed to wait before reaching that conclusion?"

"I have never stood up anyone. I'm not the sort of person who does that!"

"I hate to break it to you, but you just did it."

"I did not! I was still intending to come until I heard your message."

I snorted in derision. "So let me get this straight. You're not the sort of person who stands people up, and when you found out that your date wondered if you were standing him up when you were two hours late, you got offended and stood him up? Because you're not the sort of person who stands people up? How does that make any sense?"

"Since I was still intending to come until I got your message, it is not standing you up."

I shook my head at her logic. "That's like saying that I did not intend to knock over a glass of water, but after someone thought I was going to do it, I got offended that they thought I would do that, so I knocked the glass over to spite them. The result is the same regardless of your intention. And by the way, how am I supposed to know what your intention is if you're too busy being *gracious* to your parents to tell me, and then you never show up or answer any messages for days? My experience is still that of being stood up."

"I'm not responsible for what you experienced."

I laughed. "I'm pretty sure you are directly responsible for what I experienced."

"That was your fault, not mine."

I shook my head. "Well, we're certainly not going on another date. I can tell you that."

"I would only go if you apologized."

I was caught between disbelief, amusement, scorn, and outrage. It was just as well I found out this woman was this selfish before getting too involved with her. Lisa seemed to expect me to show her the same deference that she showed her parents. She was in for a world of hurt in dating if she didn't snap out of that one because no self-respecting person will do that. No one wants to be disrespected either, and while she seemed to do it to me by accident, the attitude behind it was so dense that I hadn't gotten her to admit that a single thing was bad about her choices, which meant she would just repeat them. There was no sense in talking to her about it anymore.

In my frustration, I knew I was going to say something "rude," so I decided to just be "gracious."

I hung up on her.

White Rocks

Few of us would imagine that an attempt at beautifying our home would result in being evicted, especially when we own it, but if we've ever lived in a community ruled by a Homeowner's Association (HOA), maybe we wouldn't be surprised after all.

It all started in 2003, when my wife and I bought our first home, a three-level townhouse that was only a patch of dirt and plans on paper at the time of purchase. We could customize it prior to construction, such as choosing an extra bathroom here, another doorway from the garage there, but there are reasonable limits on this sort of thing. We couldn't get them to paint the walls anything beyond white, and we had many customizations in mind that we had to personally do, so we had a lot of work left after moving in.

A low-priority item was the front garden, which we didn't fix until 2006. It came with an L-shaped row of green bushes framing the short walkway from the drive-way. Between those shrubs and the sidewalk was our little garden. Not being a flowers and plants kind of guy, I couldn't tell you what was there when we moved in, but even my wife disliked them. Some were short, unappealing evergreens that began to die. Others were supposedly flowers, but when a splash of color wasn't present, a mass of weed-like leaves was always there as part of it. Mulch surrounded it all, and this was what finally inspired the change that set events in motion.

A big rainstorm washed the mulch onto the sidewalk and driveway, both ours and a neighbor's. And with plants dying, we redid the entire thing except the bushes. We went all-in, even digging up the clay earth and replacing the soil. Being a recently married, first-time owner can make you care so much about these things that you spend hours of backbreaking work on them.

To solve this drainage problem, we mimicked what others in the neighborhood had done—we framed the garden with little white rocks. We also created a decorative oval of bigger stones in the garden's middle because it would match the oval window above the adjacent front door. For the oval's center, we planted a white rosebush, with four tall lilies around it. We then surrounded this with other flowers. Even I liked the result. So did many neighbors, as they often stopped to look at it and say something to us if we were outside

We were able to enjoy it a year, until May 2007, when the community HOA launched a campaign of terror. Almost 150 of the nearly 500 townhouses and single-family homes received letters about violating the neighborhood standards, with threats of steep fines if the offending item was not fixed immediately; I never learned why they suddenly did this. Virtually everything was cited. Bird baths in the front lawn. Satellite dishes. New fencing. Screen and storm doors. Portable air-conditioning units. Trellises. Trees. Repainted doors and shutters. Decks. Hot tubs. Storage sheds. Basketball hoops. Playground sets.

And white rocks in gardens.

Figure 2 The Revamped Garden

Some of these items cost hundreds if not thousands to install. Or they came with 2-year contract agreements for satellite service and penalties for early cancellation. Simply removing them wasn't as easy as the threatening letters made it seem. Adding to the offense, one house would be cited for an offending item while another had the same issue and was not. And most, if not all, of the offending items had been there for years without citation and were suddenly a problem. Even people who were cited were upset. Outrage simmered throughout the community.

The local paper caught wind of it all and sent a reporter to cover the next monthly HOA meeting, held in our clubhouse beside the pool. I may have been the reason they found out. They printed my remarks to them in the "Letters to the Editor" section in its entirety except for my last paragraph alerting them of the next meeting.

Earlier this year, The Housing Management Associates (HMA), which runs the XXX Community Association on behalf of the HOA, started a campaign of terror on XXX residents. Many have suddenly received letters of violation that some aspect of their exterior is against community guidelines. This is true even when the "transgression" has been in place as long as the house has existed—some residents with satellite dishes on their fences for over 4 years are just now receiving violation letters when they were originally told by the previous management company that the location was okay.

The other widespread offense lately is any stone work being non-earth toned. There's no such requirement in the XXX guidelines stipulating all stones must be earth toned, but this does not matter. There's a convenient catch all that HMA's Jennifer Brown explained to me (this is my particular "issue"). It says that if the guidelines do not cover your specific modifications, you must apply to the Architectural Control Committee (ACC) for the change, even if no one in their right mind would suspect trouble. A drive through XXX will show such stones everywhere in gardens.

But not for long. Many, but not all, such residents have received threatening letters to remove the stones or face stiff fines and liens against their property if compliance does not occur within as little as ten days. My immediate neighbor has stones very similar to mine but received no such violation for theirs, and this arbitrary enforcement is unfair.

The argument against the stone is that off-white stone is not a naturally occurring element of the region. Yes, as if my townhouse itself, or the blacktop, or the lamp posts are all natural elements and these off-white stones really stick out from my oh-so-natural looking street, making people think, "My God, how artificial and bizarre! Let's get out of here!" Property values must already be plummeting.

What has really upset many XXX "violators" is that our pool passes, for which we have paid, have been withheld until we comply with HMA's demands, setting off an avalanche of outrage in XXX. My first violation notice gave me 30 days to comply. Within 14 days, they withheld my passes. They didn't even wait to see if I was doing it. Outraged, I decided not to. After the second notice, I filled out their paperwork and got pointless signatures on it from my equally outraged neighbors. Everyone in my town row and several across the street are XXX violators, as if we have pink flamingoes in the yard. Since then, HMA has apparently lost my application and sent me a third nasty letter demanding I do it or be fined $100.

Another obnoxious part of this is that violators are being told to correct the violation, even while waiting to hear a decision from the ACC. Yeah, as if I'm going to dig up 10 bags of loose rocks, store them somewhere, and then put them back if the ACC says it was okay after all. Who has the time or wants to break their back repeatedly?

HMA has been obnoxious for some time and my wife and I are finally so tired of being hammered on that we are putting our house up for sale and getting out. Since we're apparently awful residents of XXX, I guess the HOA and HMA will be pleased.

By the way, on June 12th there's an HOA meeting and many neighbors, from what I hear and read on the community message board, are angry and planning to raise the issue. Unfortunately, I cannot be there due to family obligations.

Randy Zinn

When the paper came out, I was very popular on my street for a week. The paper's coverage of the meeting revealed that it was standing room only when no one was usually there except the handful of board members. After years of not bothering to enforce the community standards, leaving people to do whatever they wanted with impunity, they had come down hard on everyone with a draconian attitude. Was there a new sheriff in town?

No, but there was almost a new HOA president. I missed the meeting, but my neighbor told me that much yelling happened. It reached such a fever pitch that the current president quit and stormed out of the community clubhouse before the mob could burn it down with him inside. Two minutes later, he stormed back in and un-quit, if that's a thing. I lived in Phase 2 of the neighborhood, where Phase 1 dated back to the early 1990s. The president was one of the original Phase 1 owners and the only HOA president we had ever had, so failing to enforce community standards, and the decision to emulate a police state, were both on him. I was not alone in feeling like the Phase 1 people acted like they were better than we interlopers in Phase 2, but in this case, they targeted everyone with equal fervor.

In theory, the standards kept everyone's home values, and that of the entire community, high. Peeling paint, weeds, and other eyesores would make it harder to attract buyers for those wanting to sell. This is true, but we were watching the "letter of the law" instead of the principle of it be suddenly enforced. People were getting violation notices even when their changes would have been approved, but they hadn't done the paperwork and gone through the process. Others were not so lucky and were about to be drawn into a prolonged battle.

Many people saw nothing wrong with even their neighbor's choices when, according to the HOA, their own house value would plummet for it. Satellite dishes were not allowed to be viewed from the street, and for those who owned homes in certain locations, that meant they essentially weren't allowed to ever get one. A front door that had been painted a different color than the original was also in violation. So were shutters, or replacements that were even a slight variation (this was true even if the originals were no longer available as substitutions). Or an installed storm door. Someone actually had a list of approved storm door designs, and if yours didn't match it, you couldn't put it in.

You could not complete the purchase of a home in the community if you didn't sign paperwork indicating you would abide by the rules. That people knew about them and violated them anyway didn't abate the outrage, partly because the guidelines had no justifiable reason for existing and were the opinion of some unknown person you didn't agree with. White rocks were a good example. Show me a study proving that white rocks lower property values and I'll happily dig them up.

There was another reason people had violated the guidelines. They required all residents to get approval for certain kinds of changes, but since no one had been enforcing them, people had been assuming that something was approved. For example, we must have seen thirty houses with white rocks in their garden. In fact, one house had *only* white rocks for their garden. No plants! We had seen this for three years and assumed we did not need approval because we weren't doing anything different, aside from our decorative oval. But did the shape get us in trouble? No. The color of the rocks did.

Unhappy that we had to bow to unreasonableness, my wife and I reluctantly bought gray rocks like those of neighbors who had them and hadn't received a violation notice. We covered the edging of marble with these but left the oval in the center, sending a letter saying we had made the requested changes. We were splitting hairs. They had said our white rocks were the problem. The stones in the center were technically gray. I knew this was bullshit by me, but I really didn't want to remove my decorative oval. My wife agreed. I figured the worst that could happen would be that they would inspect and tell me "not good enough" and I would have to remove them.

Through the community message board, I met others who were fed up. Eight of us began a series of meetings in local coffee places. Our goal was to propose changes to the policies. One guy, Brad, was the owner of the nothing-but-white-rocks garden. He had already talked to a lawyer who said we needed a petition and to get 50% of the neighborhood to sign it, forcing the HOA to consider the changes.

Drunk on outrage, we repeatedly met, and I drew up the petition based on our discussions, which were productive and reasonable. But one by one, the group numbers dwindled until the last few finally admitted that they were not comfortable knocking on the doors of their neighbors. It was down to me and Brad, and even he decided he wasn't doing it, saying with a smile that he was "a beaten man" and knew when to give up. He was being fined $1000 and his wife made him stop. We must have wasted over five hours in meetings, and several more by me alone, and they were bailing on me. I was pretty upset with them, but in retrospect, I don't know what any of us were thinking.

I didn't hear from the HOA again. No news is good news, right?

My wife and I had been intending to move anyway and put the house on sale by October. Within days, HGTV called. Their show, "Get It Sold," wanted to feature our home. Their program comprised finding a house that wasn't selling, giving it a makeover, and then showing two comparison properties to indicate how it had not been measuring up to competition. They had just completed doing this on another townhouse in our neighborhood and offered to pay us $100 to film for an hour. We would be one of the comparison houses. I agreed to it, figuring "Featured on HGTV" would help me sell it. When they filmed, they even commented on how much they liked our garden, which still had the oval in the middle. Did this vindicate me for still having it? I thought so.

In February, I received a surprise bill from HMA, on behalf of the HOA, for unpaid fines of over $4500. I assumed it was a mistake. There was no explanation. They apparently expected me to just see this stunning bill and pay it without caring what it was for. I called to find out and never received a call back. A month later, I received another letter with a "Notice of Intention to Create a Lien" against my house for fines over $5000.

And I went ballistic.

I learned they were legally required to send this notice. That was probably the only reason they had bothered to tell me. This was apparently easier than returning a phone call. Or including an excuse in any correspondence. Or telling me of a fine that was escalating while they said nothing. I would soon learn there were many things they could have done prior to this but had decided to forgo. There wasn't a chance in hell I was paying for this because nothing could warrant a fine that large.

The lien would have a devastating effect on my credit score and make it impossible to secure a loan to buy another home. It would also prepare the way for them to foreclose on my home to get the money they felt I owed them, resulting in my wife and I being evicted and unable to get another home loan for up to seven years. The HOA had gone nuclear on me. But at least I found out what it was for—the rocks. How rocks could cause $5000 in fines I had yet to learn; naturally, there was no explanation until I demanded one, and the answer was hard to believe and amounted to gross stupidity and negligence on their part. And I wasn't paying for it.

I had sent a letter the previous May, telling them we had taken care of the white marble rocks they had complained about. I had left the circle of other gray rocks. They were supposed to inspect the result and tell me whether they were okay with the changes. They apparently were not.

They did not check my handiwork until October. Instead of telling me to make more changes, they fined me $100 as if I had ignored their threatening letters. This was an improper fine, which was for May. They needed to tell me they had fined me, but they didn't. They also didn't tell me they wanted more changes. Then they fined me another $100 for June, as if I had been told of the May fine and refused to pay it or make changes. They fined me another $100 for July. And then $25 a day every day after that up to October. This was all done retroactively. Then they finally told me, right?

Nope. The $25 a day fining continued through November. December. January. And into February, when someone finally sent me the cryptic $4500 bill. By that point, they had been fining me for 6 months without notification; I was only just now finding out I had been fined even once, not to mention over two hundred times. When I'd called in February to learn what the bill was for, they hadn't called back. I'm guessing they knew they stood to gain another $25 for every day they didn't bother to tell me about any of this. Then in March I got the notice to create a lien. In my snarky letter to the woman who ran HMA, I told them they could do none of this and I would see them in court. I also wrote something like, "It must be nice to operate a business where failure to do even the bare minimum of effort stands to earn substantial amounts of money. This seems like a great gig, and I wish I had thought of it myself. In fact, do you have any job openings?"

Over the next few months, they first agreed not to fine us anymore, but insisted they were right to do so because we were told to remove the rocks. This was technically not true, and documentation proved they had only said they were not approved. Obviously, I knew the implication, but I had done what I was required to do—make changes and notify them. They were the ones who had failed to inspect and tell me it was okay or to change more. We agreed to discuss it at the next HOA meeting, where I struggled to be civil. But I had learned over the years that having a powerful case against stupidity is best presented factually and without attitude. The latter weakens your argument.

In June, I presented my case so that it became clear we had repeatedly made an effort. I showed how their documentation was vague, they cited rules that didn't exist, and the required course of action was seldom specified. Legally, all of this benefited me and part of me was dying to go to court. I also wanted to call the newspaper or local TV stations with the story.

I made HMA look obnoxious and incompetent, on behalf of the HOA. Several board members agreed with me, one asking the HMA rep if they had incurred any expenses over the issue. None had been. And yet the fines, all eleven months of them, had now reached $5700 because they had continued to fine me. This was despite them having previously agreed, in writing, to stop, and knowing we were slated for this discussion. Most of them knew they wouldn't get far in front of a judge.

And so they ultimately waived all the fines. Every last one of them. However, they decided on a new fine of $100 for not getting approval in the first place. I didn't agree with this because there was a debate about whether certain things required approval, rocks being one of them. It was also an invented fine—nowhere did it say that making changes without approval would cause a fine. But I paid the $100 to make this bullshit go away. The last remaining item was doing something about the rocks.

I wasn't removing all of them like they demanded, having nowhere to store them. I just bought more mulch and buried them. It is 2021 as I write this. I still live here because we ultimately decided not to move. And the rocks are technically still there. I suppose you could say that, in a stupid sort of way, I won.

I'm Open to Suggestions

Sometimes it's good to know early that you and another person are not a good fit for each other, whether for romantic relationships, friendships, coworkers, or anything else. As my sixteen-year relationship with my then-wife was ending in 2016, I needed a new social life and had turned to Meetup.com. The site offered interesting events with the possibility of meeting someone. By June 2019, I had attended many events and dated a few women from them, but my favorite groups were shutting down. JJ ran two of them with over 30,000 people each, but he was now married with a kid and ending the groups just months after our New Zealand trip that spring (and featured in the next tale, "The Dark Whisperer").

And that led me to Lexi. She owned a sailboat, docked in Annapolis, Maryland, and she had just created a Meetup group to take people out for afternoon sailings. I had gone on cruises, ridden jet skis, and enjoyed catamarans and other boats in tropical waters, but never a sailboat. I signed up for one of her trips with four others, paid her fee, and just had to wait for the date.

With no real qualifications, anyone can join Meetup.com and create a group for a yearly cost of under

$200. This host then creates events, each with a date and time, plus a description that can vary in detail, such as requirements for guests. For example, if Lexi hosted an event at an ice-skating rink, she might say that your own skates were needed, or you could rent them at the named facility. A helpful host might reveal the going rate from that business. If skating is two hours, this duration is listed, and if the group might go to a local bar after, this is also stated, with directions and any requirements for that establishment. A smart host provides enough details on the event web page at Meetup to minimize obvious questions from group members considering attending. Being a good host is like other hosting in life—be helpful, courteous, and thoughtful.

Site users can join groups, peruse events, and sign up for free or paid ones that interest them. Paid events will have a deadline (set by the host, like everything) for paying a deposit and/or the remaining fees. The host often capped the count of attendees, which meant that if you were too late to join, you were out of luck, unless there was a waiting list (if someone ahead of you canceled). In my experience, if there's a spot, you're in, and only not paying on time gets you removed. Anyone in the group can post comments on an event page or use the site's email system to message the host. All of this is handled on the Meetup site, and you eventually attend the event, hopefully having a good time while hanging out with strangers who are typically open to meeting others.

As I waited for my sailing event with Lexi, Lexi created another, larger event for late summer, when she would charter a boat for a weekend cruise up and down the Chesapeake Bay, stopping nowhere. The charter company would supply the crew, food, and the shared cabins. The problem for the host of such an event is that if you charter the boat and not enough people sign up, you can lose a lot of money, including your deposit if you cancel.

So Lexi created a Meetup.com event that she labeled in all caps. "PLACEHOLDER." Other verbiage showed she was gauging interest before allowing anyone to book the trip and pay a deposit, but you could RSVP your interest. And many people did, so one day, Lexi updated the event to say that she was holding a "planning meeting." She also created that as a separate event on the site. She scheduled it midweek at 9pm in a bar. As a divorced father of two young children who were sometimes in my custody, I wasn't bringing little kids into a bar at all, not to mention midweek at their bedtime. But as it was only a "planning meeting," I thought I could learn the plans when she updated the placeholder event with the details and allowed people to sign up for real. The planning meeting came and went.

Over the next two weeks, people continued to RSVP for the placeholder event on Meetup, sometimes leaving a comment or asking a question. Since I had RSVP'd, I received notifications of these but never checked the site to read them. Or at least, not until Lexi responded to one.

Her note read, "Why are people still RSVPing for this?!?! Please stop. The charter is already fully booked!"

Wait. What? I thought in disappointment. The event was already gone, and I had never had a chance to sign up? How was it already booked? I carefully looked over the placeholder event page on Meetup and it hadn't changed aside from user comments. It still said "PLACEHOLDER." I still could not pay a deposit. It didn't show how many people were going because none were. There was no waiting list. There were still no details confirming anything. It didn't say the trip was planned, not to mention open for booking, or booking had completed. Judging from the barrage of surprised and disappointed comments from others who had shown interest and now saw Lexi's comment, I wasn't the only one surprised. I left my own comment on the webpage.

Rand: How is this already booked? It never opened for booking, and it still says it's a placeholder.

Lexi: It was booked two weeks ago at the planning meeting.

I frowned. Why would she book it offline? That was not how Meetup.com worked. Or at least, none of the dozens of events via various groups I was in had done that. Everything was arranged through the website. You RSVP'd, paid a deposit or the full balance, or joined a waitlist if it was full. I wondered if Meetup.com took a cut off the money as part of their business model, and she was dodging it by booking the event offline. That probably went against a policy. Part of me couldn't blame her if she was doing it, but she had kept a bunch of people out of having a shot at this. It wasn't cool, and I wanted to confirm.

R: You mean you did all the booking offline?

L: Yes.

R: Did people have to be at that event to book this?

L: Well, I knew I would take some bookings and enough people wanted to that it just filled up.

R: Not everyone can make it. This gave people like me no chance.

L: I can't help that.

I snorted. Of course she could. She had caused it! She sounded selfish and indifferent, but I tried not to say anything.

R: This is very disappointing. I would have liked to have gone.

L: Well, I wouldn't have let you book the cruise unless I had met you.

That was a little off-putting. And I wasn't sure I understood. It sounded like she was saying she rejects people based on some unknown criteria. We hadn't met, and I was already booked on her Sunday afternoon sailing, so why couldn't I have booked this one online, too? I tried to keep this simple.

R: You meeting someone first isn't included in the event post as something that must happen.

L: I thought it was obvious.

There wasn't much I could say to that. People often think something is obvious when it isn't. Was she saying I was stupid for not realizing it? Based on the other user comments, no one else knew this either. Were we all stupid? One thing was certain—it wasn't that obvious. I had noticed she wasn't the least bit apologetic, and I was starting to dislike her.

L: There will be other charters like this.

R: Can you do the planning meetings on a weekend?

L: No, I only do it midweek.

That meant I could not attend one. How was I supposed to book a charter with her? I had also noticed something else.

R: I don't see an event for the booked cruise, just this placeholder still on my calendar.

L: I didn't create one. No need.

I shook my head, laughing. By leaving the placeholder up and not creating the actual event because there was "no need," she let people think they still had a chance to sign up when they didn't. I was reserving that weekend for it just in case, only to learn now that I had been freed of that "need." She was thoughtless. As long as her needs were met, she clearly didn't care that any people in her group were awaiting an opportunity that was now gone. She should have taken the placeholder down, or put a note on it that the charter was booked offline and was now full. And she could have put up the actual event even if it was closed so people saw this. Instead, she kept us all ignorant. And she had the audacity to express disbelief and annoyance that people were still RSVPing to the placeholder. I tried to find a polite way to say something about this; we were still commenting on the temporary event page where anyone could read our conversation.

R: You should probably cancel this one. Or turn off the RSVP feature if you can.

L: Why? I want people to see I do these kinds of events.

I laughed more. Would I really have to explain that people would continue to express interest for an event that they could not attend? And if she just posted the actual event like any normal Meetup host, people would see that she did them. I tried to let it go.

R: Well, people are surprised by a lot of this.

L: I'm open to suggestions.

I left it alone for the time. No one else had chimed in on our publicly visible comment thread, maybe because I was raising many of the issues for them? This was on a

Monday and I would see her the next Sunday at the sailboat cruise. Or so I thought. Even constructive criticism is better done in person. We can see the reaction, gauge the person, and soften the tone, not to mention prevent them from reading tone into written words, as often happens. I figured it could wait a week.

But then the next day, she posted an identical "placeholder" event for another charter cruise two months later than the first one. She was going to repeat the same mistakes we had just discussed, verbatim. I couldn't believe it. She had said she was open to suggestions.

Being the fool that I am, I made my comments in a private message on Meetup, suggesting she create an actual event (not a placeholder). Give it a deadline for people to pay a deposit or full balance and make it far enough in advance that she can book the charter in time. Close the RSVPs once fully booked. I thought this was fair. It was also how events were typically done, so it wasn't like I was suggesting something weird.

I also commented on the reasons to do it this way, because she hadn't seemed to accept the pitfalls of her approach. This was apparent not only by repeating it all, but by the lack of remorse, her dismissiveness, and the bewilderment that people were not thrilled with her handling of it. This included telling people these additional requirements—she has to meet you first, you have to book in a bar midweek, etc. Recognizing that these observations were inherently critical, I tried to soften my remarks by explicitly saying I was not trying to give her grief but just improve this for group members.

But in her first response moments later, it became apparent that it didn't work.

Lexi: I don't think I'm the right event organizer and Meetup group for you.

I did a double-take. She was floating the idea of kicking me out of her group? Seriously? That was over the top. It wasn't just that I should not attend one of the charter events, but *any* of hers. Ever. Even ones that did not have these requirements. This was the result of making suggestions she had asked for. It amounted to "fuck off if you don't like the way I do things." It also seemed to imply that everyone was happy with her methods, despite the comments from others indicating otherwise, and that I had unreasonable requirements or expectations. Meetup is all about coming together, and here she was casually raising the idea to reject and expel me. I flushed and grew angry.

She continued.

Lexi: There's no way I'm going to open it and let people pay when I haven't met them. I'm definitely not spending the weekend with strangers I've never met.

That struck me as an odd thing to say, given that she was the host of events for strangers to meet. Maybe she wasn't the right person to be hosting meetups, rather than me not being the right person to be in the ones she was hosting.

Was she such a superb judge of character that a few minutes of meeting someone in a bar was enough to know that a weekend with them would be acceptable? Was everyone else that good at judging others? What if I attended the "planning meeting" and only met three of those who she agreed to let on the boat? Lexi had vetted them all, but I had not, so what if she accepted someone that made *me* uncomfortable?

It was clear before now that she only cared about herself, but what really got me was the idea of one or more people passing judgement on whether they deemed others acceptable before letting them into an event. It smelled rotten. In admitting that this was the reason she booked offline, it suggested she knew it was wrong because if someone she didn't like booked online, she might have problems ejecting them from an event without just cause. For example, what if she was racist and wanted to exclude someone black after they booked a spot? How would that look, especially if a pattern of it emerged?

I supposed that as the host, it was her right to not care what others thought of this, but hosts are not supposed to have an indifferent, selfish attitude, or they won't get repeat attendees. Saying nothing in advance about these requirements made it worse.

Her language was powerful with its "no way" and "definitely." Explicitly telling her I was hoping to not upset her had apparently been disregarded. I had poked a bear and now tried to dodge her anger.

R: Is there a difference between spending an afternoon or a weekend with strangers? I just spent nearly two weeks in New Zealand with people when I had only met one. We're all different, of course. And a boat is a little closer.

L: Yes, there's a huge difference. Most people are picky about who they sleep next to and are on a boat where they cannot just get up and leave.

While this was true, incidents happen, even between people who've known each other for decades—or a short while in a bar! This was not a guarantee of no trouble arising. And I had no say, zero, in who my roommate was on that trip, nor did anyone else who didn't go with a friend as their roommate. She was trying to say she was looking out for everyone else, but she was projecting her concerns onto other people. Lexi should not have been hosting events like this if they made her uncomfortable. Her solution of the bar smelled lamer by the minute. And then she made it worse.

R: I'm curious how you handle telling someone no if you've decided they aren't a good fit. Can imagine it gets awkward.

L: It's pretty simple when they cannot find anyone to share a cabin with.

I scowled. At these planning meetings, interested people apparently had to socialize and hit it off with someone who agreed to bunk with them. They had no idea this was true before arriving for this "planning meeting." If they failed, they were excluded, rejected. This was obnoxious. It struck a nerve for me, too, as someone who had grown up shy and with speech problems. That Lexi's profile photo showed a stunning blonde woman in an evening gown may have revealed the source of this popularity-driven attitude. I also noticed how dismissive and "not my problem after all" she was about it.

I had asked what happened if *she* decided someone was not a good fit, and she basically replied that no one else would think so either. That was egotistical. What were they going to do, freeze that person out of further interactions that night? And what if she was comfy with them, and so was their selected roommate, but someone else there was not? Did they get voted out after all? It all seemed selfish and callous, but Lexi was fine with it.

This was not like any Meetup group I had been in. I had never seen one where you couldn't just pay and go; you had to be deemed acceptable, like high school. I now wasn't sure I wanted anything to do with her or her events, including the sailing one on her personal boat the coming weekend. I thought about asking for my money back but slept on it, the conversation ending.

I looked into charters like the one she was doing and saw that they were $1600 for an overnight trip like what she had set up. She was charging over $250 per person and having ten people, so she was making $1000 on it. As someone running a group where people paid money to attend events she profited from, she had to deal with criticism. It was a business.

But it seemed that Lexi was running a group to make friends for herself with a Lexi-first approach. She was not creating events people might like with an attendee-first attitude. Most of her comments were about what she wanted for herself. And the idea that she wasn't thinking enough of her guests pissed her off. The truth hurts.

The next day, right before lunch, Lexi sent me another message, which I wasn't expecting, my guard down until I saw it.

L: I'm going to refund your money for this Sunday's sailing. Don't think this group is a good match for you.

I flushed with anger at being rejected, and her once again passive aggressively floating the idea of ejecting me from the group. But she was right. Someone who acted like this wasn't someone I wanted to be around. Feeling personally attacked, and that I had just been told to go fuck myself, I responded in kind with a final suggestion.

R: Wow, you really suck at taking suggestions, especially when you said you were open to them. Go fuck yourself.

She didn't reply, and I withdrew myself from her group. She likely reported the conversation to Meetup for my last remark, but if so, they did nothing. With any sense, they could see the context. And maybe that was why she tried to cover her tracks. I didn't know if there were rules for or circumstances that would inhibit a group host from retaliation like this, but since I wanted nothing to do with her, I didn't look into it.

On a hunch days later, I looked at her first placeholder event. She had deleted all of my public questions about what had happened and even the one where she said she was open to suggestions (liar!). She hid the comments from others where they expressed similar negative reactions on the event's page, in the comments section. She was hiding the trail of evidence that some people weren't happy with her as a Meetup host. I had ruffled her self-image and reflected back to her a version of herself that she couldn't accept, making her feel bad about herself, so she had to get rid of me. The irony was that she had made other people feel bad and would continue to do so, and she rejected my attempt to prevent that. As long as someone else felt bad instead of her...

Part of me felt bad about my last words to her, but my judgment about it was confirmed the next day, when I told a neighborhood friend about it as our kids played nearby.

"She really sucked at taking suggestions," I said.

"Especially when she asked for them."

I laughed at the shared opinion. "She kicked me out of her event next week."

"The one you already paid for? That's fucked up."

"Yeah, and then for the second time, she threatened to kick me out of the group."

"Yeah, go fuck yourself. That's what I would've said," he remarked, and I started cracking up that he had the same reaction, quoting me without knowing it.

"That was *exactly* what I wrote!"

He was laughing now. "Every guy would say that. Some people can't take any criticism, and she killed the messenger."

That sounded about right. This was something I had set myself up for before. I've always been the guy who will say something that someone else won't. I never seem to learn not to. Sometimes it makes me laugh. And sometimes I feel like a fool. But I believe in that idea to "do unto others as you would have them do unto you."

And so when I see a preventable mistake that causes problems, I want to say something. I think it's the right thing to do, and it is what I would want someone to do for me. It doesn't matter how many times it blows up in my face. I keep doing it. Maybe it's because I'm always on the lookout for that person with enough humility, decency, and self-awareness to recognize a fault and overcome it. And help me do the same. It's better than remaining exactly as we are, stuck in a self-defeating loop of mistakes we have too much pride to break out of.

And yet, was that what I was doing, repeating this behavior? If so, it wasn't pride, but a desire for something better in others and myself. I screw up. Sometimes I know it. Sometimes I have no clue. And I hate the idea that someone will just let me do it because, if they say something to stop my self-destruction, they're afraid I will turn on them as Lexi turned on me. What comes around goes around. No one will save me from myself and so therefore I should help no one else? What can't it be the other way around?

Maybe I am unconsciously testing people to learn what their character is. Is the world full of people terrified to be criticized or criticize, even constructively, because we're all so fragile? It isolates us with our faults, unable to escape them. It makes this a lonely place as we go around needlessly alienating people.

Or does it? Maybe keeping our mouth shut is the key to relationships. Would I have Lexi in my life today if I had said nothing? What is it to me if she makes people angry or feel bad? Because it's principle, and I don't think she was doing it on purpose, just being clueless, as I have so often been. But is the practical reality my problem? Yes, because it was affecting me. And would I respect her if she continued to act that way? Probably not. I wouldn't respect myself for saying nothing, either.

But at least I quickly learned that Lexi wasn't the sort of person I wanted in my life, and it was mutual. Figuring that out sooner rather than later was its own reward.

The Dark Whisperer

Not all whispers are created equal. Some amuse us. Some destroy us. Some seem like they aren't a big deal until they take on a life of their own. They grow out of control, stoke fires, burn bridges, and leave a trail of charred ash behind. Given their power, knowing the source of these dark whispers within us is vital to influencing whether they conquer us, or we conquer them.

They may originate with "life"—a series of seemingly random moments when reality clashes with expectation. And in the confused haze to follow, the dark whispers may say we have been a fool. Or maybe someone else murmured in our ear, planting a seed that grows into brambles, and pricking those who venture too close to us. For many, the worst source of dark whispers is ourselves. Insecurities awaken. Suspicions form. Doubts surge. And in a moment of weakness, they can take control, and where once stood our good-natured self, now rampages a monster born of dark whispers, cleaving a path of destruction through ourselves or all those around us.

When I boarded the first of several planes to fly from Maryland to New Zealand in March 2019, I did not know that my dream vacation would turn into something of a nightmare, courtesy of a dark whisperer in my midst. I had wanted to visit the country since the mid-1990s thanks to two shows filmed there: *Hercules: The Legendary Journeys*, and *Xena: Warrior Princess*. Most people assumed that *The Lord of the Rings*, also filmed there, inspired me, but that came later. I had often wondered where they filmed because everything looked so gorgeous, so I looked it up. I've long been a mountain man, not in that I climb them (I don't even hike anymore), but in finding them beautiful and dramatic in all their majesty. My perfect scenario would be living by a tropical, modern metropolis at the foot of a stunning mountain that wouldn't explode and kill me one day.

But since I live in the mostly flat Maryland, where the 3,000-foot-tall Sugarloaf Mountain is as impressive as it gets, I must settle for vacations to the epic grandeur of higher, snow-capped peaks, and the moody and dramatic valleys with their shadows, pines, and rushing waters. And who knows what might be hidden among them? They create a sense of adventure in me, and driving up and down the twisting roads is fun—until I get stuck behind a slow-poke who is afraid of the terrain instead of reveling in it. If you are one such slowpoke, my apologies. Also, please move over!

After two decades of occasionally lamenting that I still hadn't gone to New Zealand, especially the more dramatic South Island, I finally got my chance. On the heels of my expensive divorce, I was now used to hurling $5000 dollars at something (often month after month), and so the trip's similar price tag seemed less daunting. Besides, I had just spent a small fortune to maintain the right to see my young kids, and I felt I never should have had to spend so much. If my now ex-wife had been reasonable, I could have saved a ton. And so part of me wanted to get something wonderful for myself. Being up to my eyeballs in debt, what was another five grand?

I had joined several Meetup.com groups to rekindle my social life. Being married to the same person for about 16 years slowly shrinks that, a process aided by age and children. While I got the house in the divorce, she got the mutual friends, and these meetups were a way to get out again. One particular group had over 30,000 people and was for people in their 30-40s. A tall, skinny Asian man named JJ ran that group and another for people aged 20-30 that had 40,000 people. He organized international trips twice a year. Both groups could join, and the moment New Zealand popped up on my upcoming events, I leaped at the chance.

Before the trip, I had seen JJ at a half-dozen of his events and may have stood out around the time he announced this one. For his annual July 4th barbecue in 2018, I volunteered to grill for the 125+ guests. The other volunteer arrived and admitted she had never grilled before and didn't know how to tell when something was cooked. I pictured people getting sick or just hating burned or undercooked food and blaming JJ, and since I didn't want that and I enjoy cooking, I ended up grilling all the burgers, hotdogs, and chicken. I missed most of the event.

The pavilion layout had a concrete wall and fifteen yards separating me from everyone else, as if the designers assumed the cooks should be out of sight. When I finally finished and joined everyone, they did not see me as another guest, or as the guy who had just fed them all, but as someone not part of the event at all and who indifferently showed up hours late; I had been among the first ones there. A kind of "where did you come from? Never mind, I don't care because you aren't one of us" vibe came my way. When I mentioned what had happened to JJ as part of suggesting improvements next time, he apologized and refunded my money.

Whether or not this endeared me to JJ, I didn't know. We had also hung out a little that winter on a local group ski trip of his, but by the following March, as New Zealand loomed, I discovered that he'd chosen me as his roommate for the ten-day vacation. Recently married, his wife had just given birth and wouldn't be among the seventeen travelers. I didn't know anyone else on the trip, and JJ had a planned pre-trip dinner to help us get to know each other, but I had to miss it. Each of us had the option to have a hotel room to ourselves, but as that was more expensive, most of us had let JJ assign us a roommate. It relieved me that he'd chosen me because you never know what personality quirks someone may have. By now, both of us may have felt that the other was a safe bet. What I couldn't have known was that another guest would cause an altercation that affected me so much that multiple people would approach me to ask if I was okay.

Days 1-2 of 10

From Maryland, the trip was a grueling 22 hours, with an initial stop in L.A. An overnight flight to Fiji deposited me in an airport that seemed tiny after the behemoth that was LAX. There was no time to do anything more than gaze at tropical mountains (and sigh) before my flight to Christchurch, New Zealand. Everyone had arranged flights separately and no one else in the group was on mine, though others were more fortunate. I learned this from the texting that we began doing when killing time in various airports that included Texas, Seattle, and Australia. International texting can be prohibitively expensive, so JJ had suggested we all download WhatsApp, which was free.

I had recently purchased a small laptop and wrote on planes and while waiting in airports. Some of this was a kind of travel log, which would eventually allow me to write this account with accuracy. With help from texts, a few others in the group found me in Christchurch's airport and we waited for a shuttle (included in our trip) to the hotel.

Muted excited and impatience filled me as I chatted with them, for only long, brownish mountains caught my eye while looking out from the airport. I knew that further west beyond them, the taller peaks and deep mountain lakes awaited me days later. From the plane, I had glimpsed them, scenes from films and TV shows dancing in my head. That *The Lord of the Rings* had been one of the flight movies had only raised my anticipation, but I would need to wait.

I wasn't the only one surprised that most of our group took paid taxis to the hotel instead of our included shuttle, so I only met a handful now. Our fearless leader had been delayed and so we checked in without JJ, at a hotel that had a trolley right in the middle of an atrium that separated its two buildings. Then some of us met outside to await a shuttle to our welcome dinner, where JJ would catch up with us. It was on the street before the trolley that I had my first genuine conversations with anyone.

Emma was in her late twenties, talkative, had a nose ring, was tall, and had long, straight brown hair that had a reddish tint. She also had a slight pot belly she tried to hide by consistently pulling her purse there. Her left ankle was frequently bandaged, but she refused to say how she had hurt it. She preferred older men and wouldn't say what she did while working for an insurance company, having originally been from Chicago. She was charming in appearance and demeanor, and seemed to relish being the center of attention with her gift of gab and laid back "Ah, that's so funny!" way of bonding. She said "yeah, yeah, yeah, yeah, yeah" quickly to show she understood someone. It would soon become apparent that while Emma also had WhatsApp, she seldom checked it and was often out of the loop when we were making plans, and it might have explained why she had been on all of my flights from the U.S. after all, but had said nothing. Emma had had a room alone.

Figure 3 The Trolley

So did Adrienne, a short, energetic, somewhat bookish divorced blonde in her 30s and who always wore a hat, having brought several kinds and styles. She traveled a lot and was into herbal remedies so much that I soon joked she was a witch, which eventually became funny when she emerged from an apothecary to stand under the shop sign, which actually read, "Witchery." She told me to stop smirking. She was a talker that I clicked with enough that I realized I had to back off for fear of making her think I "liked" her. She and JJ had shared flights, and he later remarked that if he hadn't been married, something might have happened between them.

Then there was Paal, a Norwegian man in his 40s like me. He had a hearty laugh and was handsy, happy to slap a hand on your back or whack your arm with the back of his hand if you said something he found funny. He was short, had a gut and full, wavy black hair, and worked for the federal government with contracts. He was the only other one with a room to himself.

The other person important to this story is Darlene, a short, 30-something black woman with long dark braids and a tell-it-like-it-is persona. She worked as a nurse and had five brothers and one sister, took no shit, and was down-to-earth, astute, and candid. Like me, she both enjoyed and was skilled at innuendo so that we quickly became partners in smarmy comments. Others joked that we had a thing going, and if I had been attracted to her, we might have. At one point I backed off from this to avoid making her think I meant something by it. She had an overweight, black, female friend as a roommate, and while the friend loudly laughed over our innuendo, she didn't take part and seemed content to listen more than talk.

The rest of those on our trip made us an eclectic mix. Most of our 17 were singles, with only one apparent couple. I was the tallest, blond, and had a newly grown black beard to go with my decades-old mustache and goatee. I tend to be laid back, approachable, and quiet from two decades of speech problems that were long gone, but which seem to make me prone to saying things in ways that others misinterpret. But I'm quick to make a joke or comment when I have one. I place a premium on those who are logical and fair like me, partly because people who aren't have caused me no end of upset, and that's exactly what would happen on this trip.

Aside from JJ, I knew nothing about the others that first night as ten of us stood on the sidewalk awaiting our shuttle to dinner, where our travel agent would meet us. We chatted about our trip so far and what we were looking forward to. I took the photo of the trolley while standing there. As we waited, two beefy local men approached and talked to Emma and Susan for a few minutes, but I wasn't listening. When they walked away, Susan laughed.

"That was really weird," she said, one hand on her prodigious belly. She seemed friendly and wore her long blonde hair in a ponytail.

"I know, right?" said Emma, laughing and watching them go.

I asked, "Why? What happened?"

"They asked for our bras," replied Susan, chuckling.

I did a double take, almost not sure I had heard her right. How did two strange men have the chutzpah to walk up to two women on a street and ask for their bras? It was bizarre, creepy, and made me wonder if our hotel was in the wrong part of town. I asked, "What? How did that come up?"

"I don't know," Susan said. "They just asked."

"Out of the blue? They didn't offer to buy you a drink first?" I joked.

A grinning Emma asked, "Is this a thing here? Should we expect to be asked for a bra everywhere we go?"

"Apparently," replied Susan.

"I would've punched him in the mouth," said Darlene, her black braids swinging as she shook her head in disapproval, though she seemed amused.

"Yeah, that's weird," said Adrienne, not looking amused as she adjusted her hat. "Not doing that."

"Sooooo," I began, "just to clarify, would now be a bad time to admit I was going to ask for your bras?"

Darlene smirked. "That depends. Are you handing over your jock strap first?"

I feigned an apologetic smile and joked, "Sorry. I'm commando."

We all had a friendly laugh as the incident became an ice breaker. When our shuttle arrived, it proved to be a tour bus driven by Steve, who would be our driver for the first half of our journey, both around Christchurch and up to a small town, Kaikoura, and back again. He was a divorced man in his late 50s, quiet, mousy, mumbled when he spoke, and wasn't terribly exciting, but he was pleasant and cooperative. We learned that a significant earthquake had struck the city a few years earlier and was very much recovering from this. In fact, our later guided bus tour of the city was mostly a showing of damaged buildings, adding a somewhat depressing tone to the outing. Most of us concluded the city was not much of an attraction for us. This did not surprise me, as it seemed like the airport was the primary reason we were there.

For dinner, we occupied a back room at the restaurant, tall stools and tables before us. Our sampling of food included local varieties of cheese, breads, fried foods, and pastries as appetizers, all prepared in ways that made me wonder if this was specific to the country or the establishment. The most noteworthy moment came from Susan's roommate, Janice. Short and stocky with a big face and long blonde hair, she was in her upper 30s and caked in heavy, bright make-up. A girly-girl who loved pink, she brought high heels everywhere and changed into them for a photo and then back to more sensible footwear for the terrain. She was loud, belched without apology, and had little sense of things she shouldn't say, like the infamous moment at this dinner.

Figure 4 Partially Destroyed Church in Christchurch

"Where can we see a kiwi?" she asked, meaning a bird.

"Oh, I wouldn't get my hopes up," said our travel agent, a tall, middle-aged blonde woman who spoke with a noticeable English accent. "I've lived here all my life and have never seen one. They are very reclusive."

Janice said, "That sucks. I really wanted to see one. They should just be put in cages in every restaurant or something so people can see them. Just hang them up in a corner or something."

I looked at her in alarm. Suggesting this happen to the national bird of a country could offend locals. Others wore similar expressions, and the group had gone strangely quiet, as if aghast. Our host said nothing, and JJ discreetly changed the subject. The moment became one we referenced often during the trip, because Janice would say other things she shouldn't, but she clearly did not know she was making gaffes. Even the guys said her remarks embarrassed them.

We all went to bed early that night after the long flights. But JJ warned me he had a nasty stomach bug that made him unable to eat anything and keep it down. It was highly contagious and now I was sharing a room with him! At my suggestion, we consistently divided the bathroom so that he used anything on the left, like a towel, and I used the one on the right. This prevented accidental sharing and somehow, I avoided catching it. Halfway through the trip, he got past the illness, which may have been one reason he skipped most social activities beyond the pre-planned ones where he needed to host.

Days 3-4 of 10

Our first full day included sightseeing Christchurch and the earthquake damage via our bus. Steve took us to a nearby beach where Emma and I walked around together for about ten minutes. When she removed her shoes and an ankle brace to walk in the surf, I went to explore a huge outcropping of rock with a tunnel-like cave running through it, a building atop it. We also visited botanical gardens and finally a museum, most of us concluding there wasn't much to see in town. I fidgeted for something grander and felt like this was a waste of a day, but at least I know that if I ever visit the country again, I'll be skipping the city.

At the museum, I noticed Paal hanging out with Emma a lot, my impression being that he was interested in her. That idea escalated later, after JJ and I joined a handful of others for dinner. We learned that a pair of Asian women who were rooming together as friends preferred dive bars, which Emma shared, so they had gone off together, Paal joining them. But then the Asians left Emma alone with Paal, who played pool together, drinking. We would eventually learn that he was hitting on her, which didn't surprise us, but it eventually became more of a she said/he said issue when her credibility came into question.

The next day, we checked out of the hotel and boarded the bus to Kaikoura to the north, a three-hour drive that included a stop at a local winery. As often happens, people became creatures of habit and sat in certain areas of somewhere like a bus. JJ, I, and Emma were among those preferring the back, causing some hanging out with each other and storytelling. Emma asked about what sorts of books I wrote and published and about my divorce and kids.

She also joked about cruel things she had done to people who she felt had it coming, offering examples. This included a guy who wouldn't take no for an answer, so she began leading him on, breaking dates, and finally standing him up until he relented. A co-worker who did sloppy work asked her to look over documents, and on seeing the errors, Emma decided not to fix them so the peer would get in trouble for it and learn the hard way to shape up. This inspired us to joke about not getting on her nasty side, JJ nicknaming her Evil Emma.

I found her entertaining, and while the group tasted wines and sat around on the winery's patio together, talk turned to everyone gathering that night at the motel for drinking. Emma liked the idea despite having not bought any varietals, so I joked that none of us were going to let her drink our wine. She bought herself two bottles after that.

We filed back onto the bus and soon stopped for lunch at an uninspiring roadside deli, the poor fare triggering some of us to walk to the convenience store next door for other options. I was among these and found some crackers to go with the wine. For cheese, I only had two options and couldn't decide between them.

"Are you really buying that huge thing?" Emma asked in disbelief, having apparently followed me over. She stood beside me, eyeing the giant chunk of cheese in my hand. It was two inches high, four inches wide, and about seven inches long. And that was why I didn't want to buy it, but the only other choice was slices designed for sandwiches.

"I haven't decided. It's way too much for just me. Maybe if everyone helps me with it."

"Oh, I'll help eat it. I'm from the Midwest so cheese is kinda my thing."

I sighed. "Yeah, okay. Hopefully everyone will help tonight during our little party. I grabbed crackers."

"Nice."

We went our separate ways and soon joined everyone on the bus. An hour later, the group arrived near Kaikoura, a small, rural, seaside town on the east coast, the Pacific Ocean stretching to the horizon. White-capped mountains loomed in the distance, smaller, brown ones nearer, much of the land a greenish brown of low grass dotted with stands of trees. I felt the excitement of seeing what I had come for—gorgeous nature that made you think *I can't believe I'm here.*

We saw seals along the shore from our winding, narrow road, but they were tough to spot on the giant boulders in the crashing surf, which lay over thirty feet below the road.. Our driver stopped south of town, suggesting we hike a peninsula trail along the coast. It would bring us nearer to town and he'd pick us up on the other end. We all agreed and got ready, bringing water, hats, and donning suntan lotion, but Emma was staying behind due to her ankle. We reluctantly went without her, climbing up steep steps and slopes for a cliff-side view of the sea.

Figure 5 At the Kaikoura Cliffs

The others took a breather at the top and I went down ahead of them to the rocky shore that extended over a hundred yards toward the sea, enough for tall grass to form on the earth, paths winding through it. A tall mound of earth provided yet another lookout, but I went past it, a hunch telling me I might find seals beyond the tan rocks that were a challenge for a secure foothold. And I was right.

I became the first to find the seals up close, all of them below me as I stood on a ledge they couldn't reach. It allowed an amazingly close look while keeping a safe distance and not disturbing them, though they watched me as if bored. I took photos and selfies before the rest of the group caught up with me after many gestures from me to come over. None of them seemed interested in joining me for the longest time and I think they would have missed all of it were it not for me.

By that time, I'd been there ten minutes and had finished, so I was among the first to walk away, but not before someone freaked out. Roz was a moody, troubled Latina in her 30s who wore a perpetual scowl and her long brown hair in a ponytail. She revealed a deep, emotionless voice the rare times she spoke. While away from the group but within sight of us, we had already seen her talking to herself and gesturing, and her roommate eventually revealed that Roz admitted to sometimes hearing voices. We all thought she had been abused. Despite all of this, she seemed nice if we could just get her to relax a little, but she skipped virtually all social activities like dinner, few of us interacting with her much. She shared a room with Dot, a short, friendly woman who had never met Roz before but revealed that the latter had anxiety that Dot was helping her with.

As we stood on the jagged rocks watching the seals, a bee began checking us out. Roz was apparently deathly afraid of them, screaming, waving her arms, and even violently swinging her backpack at it. The rest of us kept telling her to calm down because she was doing exactly the sort of behavior that gets you stung. And none of us wanted to get stung because of what she was doing. As if all of this wasn't bad enough, she wasn't standing still while doing this, nor was she watching her step as she screamed and screamed, moving this way and that. I imagined her clobbering someone else with that backpack and knocking them off the ledge and onto rocks below, or into the sea.

I was already walking away when this began the first time, and when it resumed because the bee had returned while I was still close enough to hear the screams, Darlene was not far behind me. From a distance we watched and listened to round two of the Roz freak out as we continued walking away, looking back as we picked our path on the rocks.

Figure 6 Selfie with the Seals at Kaikoura

"I'm getting away from *that* shit," said Darlene, about ten paces behind.

I laughed, and I could tell from her reaction to this that she knew at once that I completely agreed with her. This was the moment we bonded in our mutual refusal to be involved in a disaster waiting to happen. "I'll race you."

"Done," she said, laughing.

"She's doing exactly the wrong thing."

"Crazy bitch."

I knew she wasn't trying to be mean. "She's gonna knock someone down besides herself."

"She already fell once."

I winced, imagining painful scrapes and bruises. "Did she?"

"Yeah. I ain't helping her either." When I laughed, she added, "I'm a nurse. People are always trying to get me to help them when they get cut or whatever, like that's even the kind of nursing I do. Every time, Rand. I went on vacation for a break from that, not to do it when someone is being stupid."

We continued on and soon separated. One by one, the group eventually made it to the parking lot where Emma waited on a retaining wall, the bus and our driver nearby.

"Did you see any seals?" Emma asked me, so I sat next to her and showed the photos on my smart phone.

"You never would've made it with your swollen ankle. The ground wasn't exactly stable half the time. It was sometimes loose rocks that moved when you stepped on them. I wouldn't be surprised if someone else hurt their ankle out there."

We headed into town minutes later, my good mood elevated now that I had enjoyed my first taste of why I had come there. We mostly saw a single strip of a two-lane road with a parking lot at the south end, and a sharp curve away from the sea at the other. Restaurants and touristy stores lined both sides. We initially drove through on our way to the motel, which wasn't far and was a single story, a long building with a gravel driveway and parking lot. The end nearest us was apparently the bar and restaurant, which I didn't realize until wheeling my luggage over that gravel and onto a patio that ran from the end to the back, where tables with umbrellas awaited us. We filed inside and slowly got our room keys at the empty bar, my impression being that we were the only guests, though a few cars were out front. JJ insisted I always carry the lone key for our room if we ever got only one, because he had too many things to worry about and didn't want to lose it. And he had reason to worry.

From the bar and dining area, a single door led into a narrow hall, where we passed a door on either side, presumably to guest rooms, but I soon suspected that motel staff spent the night there in case any guests needed something. Then came a lobby to our left, though it looked nothing like a lobby, just a wider part of the hall. I passed by it repeatedly before realizing that it was the actual front entrance to the place. We never used it unless checking out.

The hall continued beyond, with three more guest rooms on the left. At the hall's end, we took a slight dogleg to the right, going through a glass door, and found ourselves outside at the motel's rear, the rest of it extending to our left in a straight line from the main building. It looked like a later addition. A covered veranda extended the length of it. Pairs of wooden seats, with an attached table between them, sat outside each room's sliding glass rear door. We only used these entrances, not the front doors. A tall hedge of various bushes as tall as me ran along the veranda. The hedge had a single break in it to a wide lawn, beyond which were trees and an excellent view of the snow-capped mountains.

As JJ and I gathered in our room, he cursed in his very understated way, holding a piece of paper. "The woman we booked the trip through screwed up the dolphin encounter tomorrow morning and we can't do it."

I picked up my copy of the note on the other bed. According to the travel agent, she could usually call just weeks ahead to book our wild dolphins swim, which took place in a nearby cove we had just hiked past. But someone had placed a new cap on the number of people allowed in the water at once. This meant reservations needed to be made months earlier. She had screwed up. Now we would be allowed on the boat, but not in the water. A highlight of the trip was gone, with only a pathetic partial refund to show for it. I felt frustrated and powerless to do anything about it, alternating between trying to let it go and feeling sour. I had once been in the water with a lone dolphin in captivity, in a carefully controlled environment, but swimming with scores of wild ones in the ocean was infinitely grander. And now something I had to watch others do instead of me. Sometimes it takes an effort to avoid irritation.

Figure 7 View from the Motel

As JJ quietly fumed, Darlene knocked on our door, insisting I come with her and practically dragging me by one arm to her room, not explaining what was so urgent until I was inside, her roommate smirking at me.

"I need you to kill these," Darlene said, pointing to two gigantic spiders high on the wall. She was too short to reach them. It wasn't the first time being 6'3" had gotten me volunteered for something. To my grin, she slightly smiled about how overly serious she was, as if warning me not to poke too much fun. The no-nonsense tough girl was apparently afraid of spiders and was going to kill me if I teased her.

"The first two are free," I joked, whacking them one by one with a newspaper, then picking them up and flushing them down the toilet when she indicated the garbage was not good enough. "After that, I require wine as payment."

"Done. Thank you, Rand!"

"Uh-huh." I walked out.

"Not a word to anyone!"

We soon boarded the bus back to town and filed into a restaurant as a group. We noticed a pattern in some parts of New Zealand—after being seated and seeing a menu, a server did not come by for our orders or bring us the pre-pared food. Instead, we had to get up and order our meal at the bar. Then we needed to wait around and get our food and carry it back. Emma and I went up together and, seeing her behind me, I gestured for her to go first. When she got her dinner, she waited for me to get mine and we returned together. This place had our group squeezed into two large, U-shaped booths, where I found myself between Emma and Darlene. Somewhere along the way, the sexual innu-endo started, with me, Darlene, and Emma leading the charge. It began due to another restaurant in town— Groper Garage.

Grouper is a type of fish, but in Australia and New Zea-land, they spell it without the letter "u," which results in the word "groper." And to grope means to put your hands on some in a sexualized way without their permission. I didn't know about this alternate spelling, but correctly guessed at it from the symbol of a fish as part of the logo. This triggered a round of jokes about what was really going on in that place. Most of us were joking like, "I wonder what goes on in there," or "Do they have a two gropes for the price of one coupon?" But Emma latched on to repeat-ing one of several versions of the same idea:

"I really wish someone would grope me."

"I wonder what it's like to be groped."

"Can someone show me what being groped feels like?"

"Yeah, I just came in to be groped. Thanks!"

She sometimes said these while looking at me, giving the impression she was flirting with me, albeit awkwardly. She seemed to spend time with me, just as I did with her. I had so far found her to be among the most entertaining on the trip. If any mutual interest existed, we had most of the ten-day trip ahead of us to find out, with 10-14 hours a day together in a group, so there was no rush. As usually happens on such an outing, you hang out with different people in the course of a day, slowly gravitating toward some. For me this was Emma, Darlene, and Adrienne, with a little JJ and Paal thrown in.

Many at our table that night took part in the jokes about groping or laughed about it, but there came a point where we had all moved on and Emma hadn't, returning again and again to the idea. Me and Darlene exchanged a look about this, as did others, because Emma's obsession became noticeable. While we never discussed it, I was certain we increasingly thought the same thing—she really needed to stop saying that. I had never heard a woman joke about wanting to be groped, a form of sexual assault. Didn't she realize this was bad?

There's an idea that if someone makes the same joke too many times, maybe they mean it. While I didn't think Emma wanted anyone to grope her, someone else could get the wrong impression, and in time, she said this when other people outside our group were around. What if she had said it in front of those two locals who had asked her and Susan for their bras? Emma was setting herself up. She was making me uncomfortable, and I knew I wasn't the only one.

Men are acutely aware of not setting ourselves up for uncomfortable misunderstandings. And here was Emma, barreling right into and past all sensibilities about it. But men won't admit to being uncomfortable. It's considered unmanly. That we have all felt that way is not something we admit to on pain of death. The only scenario that comes to mind, when a guy will immediately show being uncomfortable, is when another guy is nude, and a show of not being okay with that is supposed to ward off any appearance of being homosexual. Put another way, a man who is unfazed by another man's nudity—or even just his penis—might be gay. It's nonsense, but there it is.

I felt certain that the laughter greeting yet another repetition of "I wish someone would grope me" from Emma was increasingly strained. But no one said anything, not even, "Yeah, it's not funny anymore."

During our time in town, we noticed that many of the stores closed early, by 6 or 6:30 pm. This didn't affect me, but several women wanted to shop and could not. A few restaurants also seemed to close early. As we drove out of town that night, we rounded a sharp corner, at the end of which was a stop sign and a sushi place. I love sushi and always try to have some on vacation as a treat, so I was already hoping to convince someone of this for tomorrow, when we'd spend the entire day in Kaikoura or the ocean just offshore.

We returned to the motel and entered the same way as before, filing down the narrow hallway in a straight line. Emma's room proved to be one of those inside off the hall, as I learned when she stopped to let herself in, me and others passing her.

Without stopping, I asked, "Are you still coming out to drink?"

"Yeah, definitely!"

"Okay. See you out back."

Others likely heard this, and we had all talked about doing so earlier at the winery, but no one said anything about joining us, though I figured they would anyway. I continued to my room and opened one of my two wine bottles and both boxes of crackers because I expected more than just Emma. From the room fridge, I grabbed my giant hunk of cheese, which I jokingly named George; it was so big that it deserved recognition and possibly citizenship. Then I poured myself a glass and remarked to JJ, who was settling in for the night and texting with his wife back home, "I'm heading out to drink with Emma."

"Nice. She's really cute. She has a room to herself. I expect to not see you back until tomorrow."

I laughed, surprised he thought that would happen. Did he think I was some sort of lothario who could easily seduce someone? I wasn't actually trying to. Or did he think Emma was that interested in me? Any signs had been subtle aside from the groping comments, but I was writing those off. Was that a mistake? Was I clueless? I had a long history of it, for sure, but I couldn't wrap myself around the idea that she had really meant something by it. I mean it was the crude sort of flirting a guy would do and I thought only we were that dumb. Now I didn't know what to think but wasn't worried about it.

I exited the room to find Emma trying to find me and what room I was in, a glass and a wine bottle in her purse. A few others in the group were milling about; my impression was that they had tried to help her find my room before I showed up. Since my hands were full, she grabbed two white lawn chairs for us and we headed out through the hedge opening onto the lawn, then moved a few paces over so that any motel staff who passed by wouldn't see us out there drinking; signs were everywhere warning us we weren't allowed to drink any alcohol on the premises, even in our rooms, unless we bought it there.

As we were doing this, Adam saw us and grabbed a third chair. A chubby self-professed geek, he wore a long, scraggly brown beard, his mustache doing little to hide stained, crooked teeth. He often volunteered that he never dated and had no friends in his late twenties, spending all personal time playing video games. With the sexual innuendo flowing between others, he would volunteer, "I don't have to worry about that." His penchant for joking about his lame personal life, with a mixture of matter-of-factness and self-pity created the impression he was a virgin. Despite this, he was likeable but quiet, fading into the background.

He shared a room with a short Asian guy in his late twenties, with a scruffy black beard. He was thin despite eating like a pig at every meal, rapidly chewing with his mouth open and absorbed in texting his girlfriend back home, an activity he seldom wasn't doing. I once saw him still doing it while peeing at a public urinal. While he was friendly, he clearly wasn't interested in any of us. No one knew where he put all the food.

Someone else grabbed the fourth chair, and it ended up being Adam, me, Emma, and the other person sitting in a line, the hedge behind us, snow-capped mountains in the distance, a clear night sky above. I had heard that the moon is upside down in the southern hemisphere and that some constellations can only be seen there, so I used an app to identify heavenly bodies, though Mars was easily detected with the naked eye, red as it was.

Over the next two hours, a half dozen others sometimes joined us, often replacing each other as they left to get some wine or a jacket or retire for the night. They had to stand across from us because there were no more chairs. Only Emma ate the cheese and crackers with me, despite me offering it to others. We all talked of whatever came up, Emma learning I had released five music albums on my own record label. When she said she'd like to hear it, I turned on my phone to play one acoustic guitar song, but I ended up letting that entire album and my classical guitar one play as background music.

One of those who came out to stand before Emma was Paal. By now, some of us had talked about his apparent interest in her, and he now made a play.

"Can I try some of your wine?" he asked, seeming a little fidgety, as if he meant more than what he said. Then he added, "I didn't buy anything, and the bar is closed."

"Um," began Emma, "yeah. I mean, I guess. I don't have another glass."

It was obvious that her actual answer was no, but Paal didn't take the hint. I'm no genius, but I've learned over the years that women rarely say what they mean, not because they're screwing with guys, but to avoid confrontation. We're supposed to figure out what they're getting at. The problem is that guys are not only more literal, but we're looking for any sign of a way forward, being optimists. It reminds me of a scene in *Dumb & Dumber*, where Jim Carrey's character asks the woman how much of a shot he's got with her. When she says one in a million, (i.e., he stands very little chance), he gets excited and enthusiastically responds, "So you're saying there's a chance!" While that's extreme, it underscores the way men think. Hedge about sharing the wine and cite a problem that prevents you from doing so? We'll solve that! It's a yes!

Paal eagerly solved the problem Emma had raised. "Oh, I can get a glass from the room. Hold on." He strode away, and no sooner was he out of sight than Emma turned to me.

"He's really making me uncomfortable," she confided, loud enough for the others to hear. They listened to our conversation.

I wasn't sure what to say. "I'm sorry. What's he doing?"

"The other night we were playing pool, and he said three different times that if he was ten years younger, he'd be hitting on me."

I had heard this line before from male characters in 1980s TV shows when growing up. They always seemed to think it was a compliment. I hadn't considered how a woman viewed it, but I was suddenly glad that it wasn't among the foolish things I had ever said.

"Yeah, once would be one thing, but three times is weird," I agreed. I wasn't sure if she was telling the truth only because he didn't seem at all creepy to me. Was she exaggerating? Was this her way of vocalizing what we all sensed, that Paal was interested in her, but she did not share the feeling? Part of me felt bad for him that she had just said this to me where others could overhear it.

She tore into my cheese chunk with one hand, as I had no knife. "He also keeps finding reasons to touch me."

I frowned, having known a guy who did far worse. He had once taken my left wrist and, before I knew what he was doing, placed my hand on the breast of the woman we were talking to. "That's not cool," I said, once again wondering if she was making that up. He seemed too polite for that.

"I really don't want to give him any of my wine."

I nodded in the dark. That would encourage him. "Then don't."

"I already said yes."

"Not really. You said no, and he didn't take the hint. Just tell him you changed your mind." I gave her a couple other ideas and when Paal returned, she used a different excuse, saying it was all she had because she was saving the other bottle for someone back home. His disappointment was plain, and I saw he had gotten the message this time. He clearly viewed the acceptance of her sharing it with him as a sign of her interest, and now this came back as rejection. I felt bad for him as he awkwardly stood there with an empty and useless glass that now represented a rejection done in front of a half-dozen witnesses. He left before long and didn't return. In the days that followed, he no longer hung around Emma, a fact that JJ and I discussed once. My impression was that people had been talking about it for days and I sympathized with the mixture of eye rolling and pity sent his way for hurt feelings.

Eventually it became too cold as temperatures dropped. The first three out there—me, Emma, and Adam—were the last three to leave, Adam going first, so that I was alone with her for a few minutes.

"Well, we need to get up early tomorrow," she said, rising.

I started gathering my things. "Yeah, should be a good day. Maybe we can do this again tomorrow night."

"Definitely. Thank you for hanging out with me."

"Of course."

"Here, let me get that," she offered, grabbing one of my cracker boxes. My hands were full.

"Thanks. Just bring it out tomorrow night."

"Yep."

Then we parted at the veranda, her going left toward the glass door and interior hall, and me headed right along the back, past the wooden chairs and tables and sliding glass doors toward my room. As I entered, JJ was still awake in bed and deadpanned, "I'm very disappointed."

"Quit," I said, laughing. Then I realized he was serious and had expected me to get laid. Was I missing something? I suddenly felt the need to justify my failure, having had no idea I had failed to do something until he made me feel that way. Part of me felt annoyed by that, as I had made no attempt at seducing Emma. I especially would not have after her comments about Paal. Seducing an uncomfortable woman wasn't my thing. I explained lamely, "We had a lot of company."

"No excuse. You need to get her alone."

I didn't see how that could happen at this tiny motel, so while my interest in her grew, I wasn't seriously thinking to pursue it anytime soon. We had days of hanging out ahead of us, so there was no rush. I was also trying to be polite, so I only said, "Not sure that's possible."

Day 5 of 10

In the morning, JJ and I were ready to start the day, which would begin with breakfast in town, then the altered dolphin event, and conclude with whale watching from a boat. He had talked to the tour organizer to express his upset about the goof and get us a better compensation. The woman had offered a free dolphin event in the future, but JJ rightly pointed out we lived 5,000 miles away and likely weren't coming back soon. He learned that other groups we didn't know would be on the boat, and if someone from another one canceled their participation in the water, one or more of us might get to go in after all.

"How am I supposed to choose who gets to do that?" he asked me rhetorically, but an idea immediately popped into my head.

"Well, Emma was the only one who couldn't do the hike yesterday, so maybe she's the only one goes swimming with dolphins."

He looked surprised. "That's actually a good idea. A great one. I think I'll do that."

The group soon rode the bus into town and JJ announced this idea over the speaker without attributing it to me. I would not have cared except that half of the women on the bus started commenting on how nice and sweet JJ was, and how he was such a good tour host. I wryly smirked about him taking credit for my thoughtfulness via a sin of omission and having the women think highly of him for it. The irony. It wasn't cool, but whatever. Was there a petty way I could get back at him for that? Maybe I could push him overboard like it was an accident.

It proved a moot point because no one canceled, but as we milled about inside the dolphin encounter business after breakfast, waiting to get started, he revealed that he would tell Emma that the idea was mine, thinking this would raise her interest in me. In a moment of foolishness, I wondered if he was right and didn't dissuade him, but as he walked away to do it, I suddenly wished he wouldn't. But it was too late, as he was already doing it across the room as I inwardly groaned.

Was it good or bad for her to know? My suggestion had nothing to do with her personally. It was logic, not sentiment. But JJ telling her this way likely suggested that it was personal, meaning I was showing that I cared about her. That was ridiculous, given we'd known each other only two full days now, and it could be off-putting given how little we really knew each other. A man who cares too early is not attractive, no matter how movies make it seem like all a man has to do to make a woman fall in love with him is profess his love. It is fairytale nonsense. Who was a bigger fool, Paal, JJ, or me? We were all hopeless. It was a wonder any of us managed to reproduce (I don't know if Paal had kids or not). Emma did not acknowledge in any way that she knew.

Once out on the water, my excitement grew despite the situation. The hundreds of wild dolphins around the boat soon stunned us, and very jealous of other groups who could swim with them for over an hour. It was torture and took an effort to enjoy what we could without resentment.

The dolphins swam with us as they both changed positions, often leaping ahead of the bow as I had seen on nature shows.

Figure 8 The Wild Dolphins

After the boat docked, we boarded a shuttle back to town. Emma was among the last to board and one of the few available seats was next to me, so she took it. She didn't seem awkward around me, so if JJ revealing my idea to her bothered her, I didn't see a sign of it. After a lunch in town, we boarded our bus for a quick ride to the whale watching center and a large boat to go out onto the ocean with. This lasted for quite a while and we were lucky enough to see several whales blow water into the air and then do a dive with the well-known image of their tail breaching the water. I had always wanted to see this and shared excitement with my peers. It's great when hopes are fulfilled. It proved to be just what I had dreamed of, and I was very glad for the time in Kaikoura.

After we docked, I bought my two young kids some souvenirs, which weren't the first I had purchased, so I was done shopping for a few days. But the others wanted to do that when we took the short ride back to town and walked among the shops and restaurants. I had joked a couple times during the day that, with whale watching and the dolphin encounter, we should eat sushi for dinner because seafood was the theme of the day. I made this comment to no one in particular, but I made a note of who agreed, which was quite a few, and included Emma. The bus parked at one end of the strip and the sushi place was at the other, so I meandered in that general direction with anyone still going there. People peeled off as we went so that it finally became just four of us: me, Emma, and the two Asian dive bar enthusiasts.

Both of the Asians were in their 30s, like most of our group. They seemed game for anything fun or with live music or drinks. They often skipped our get-togethers to do those ASAP and late into the night. Both were tall, with long black hair, and almost perpetually wore big, black sunglasses outside, carrying very large purses. They sat together everywhere they went, often talking to each other much more than the rest of us, but they were friendly.

The three of them entered a store as I waited on the sidewalk. Suddenly I remembered how early places closed and I wondered when the sushi place would, so I hurried around the corner to it. They were closing in just thirty minutes. I strode back, partly to avoid the others coming out on the street and walking away without me, possibly leaving me unaware of where they had gone. I would end up eating dinner alone, not that I really cared. I was a loner from those decades of speech problems, but I was in a decidedly social mode for much of the trip

But they hadn't left. As I arrived at the store they had been in, Emma exited the door and descended the few steps toward me, the others ten feet behind her and look-ing nearly ready to come out, too.

"Hey," I began, "that sushi place is closing in a half hour if you still want to go."

"Um, okay. Let's ask the others." She turned around to see them approaching the exit.

"Yeah, of course."

Figure 9 A Whale Dives

The Asian women stepped out, and when Emma asked them, they enthusiastically agreed. The four of us headed over there, but no sooner did we set foot in the place than we decided there was no way we were eating there. The afternoon sun had been beating the windows to super-heat the noticeably warm air, and we noticed they had prepared the sushi in advance, sitting in that hot air for who knows how long. Eating raw fish can be risky if it's not fresh, and heat promotes bacteria forming. We left in less than a minute, and it only took that long to avoid such a hasty retreat that it gave offense. As we walked back toward the street corner, Emma and I were in front, the others behind, but when we reached the turn, we noticed that the two Asians had disappeared.

"Were they abducted by aliens just now?" I joked.

Emma laughed. "I think I would have heard something."

"Seriously, though. Where did they go?"

"Maybe into that dive bar. We're into those."

Not being into bars much, I wasn't sure what a dive bar was. "What's the draw?"

"I don't know. They're just seedy, mysterious, and unique."

"Okay." I pictured the sort of bars that fights take place in during movies, though maybe that wasn't really what she meant. But I thought women avoided such places as if they were unpredictable and dangerous, so this explanation fell flat for me and I didn't know what else to say.

"We'll give them a few minutes. Need to figure out somewhere to go for dinner."

I knew several people had talked about visiting a now infamous place and suggested we join them. "There's always Groper Garage. I think a bunch of us went there."

"I'm in the mood to be groped," she said, laughing. Then she glanced at me, adding, "I really want someone to show me what being groped feels like."

The image of my hands feeling her breasts, butt, or crotch forcibly leaped into my mind and I grew very uncomfortable. If this was her way of flirting, it was terrible and unsettling. She was lucky I had better sense than to do it, but God help her if she did this with the wrong guy. She was virtually asking to be sexually assaulted. Did she have no sense at all, or was she just reckless? She had made this joke nearly two dozen times by now, mostly the night before, but several times today each time we had passed the place. Finally, I couldn't bite my tongue any longer and said what I'd been thinking for a long time, partly to stop her from ever saying it to me again.

"You know," I began, forcing a light tone as if I still thought she was just kidding, "you should probably stop saying that before someone takes you seriously and does it."

Emma didn't respond, and moments later, the Asian women joined us, and we walked back toward the bus. Emma and I continued on until they stopped at an Indian place to eat, and she and I ended up at Groper Garage, looking for anyone else in our group, which we found at two adjacent, large tables. As usual, we needed to order at a bar, but this time we got a plastic card with a number on it and could return to a table, placing the card in a vertical holder that could be seen from a distance, a server bringing our order over. I had ordered first this time and joined the others without Emma, who I left at the bar. She soon came and sat next to me instead of taking one of the other seats. Her ankle was now bothering her and several of us suggested she elevate it with some ice, and she did.

After dinner, everyone boarded the bus back to the motel, where we silently entered the usual way, going down the narrow hallway. As I passed the lobby, I noticed Paal ahead of me going into the first room on the left. At the same moment, Emma was entering the next room down and the thought popped into my head, *She probably doesn't like his room being next to her if he's making her uncomfortable.* I continued to the veranda and then into my shared room with JJ.

Once there, I saw my wine opener and realized no one had discussed plans of what to do next. It had been a long day. Maybe no one wanted to hang out, but I knew we were headed back to Christchurch and the airport for a quick flight to Queenstown, and I had an open wine bottle with a glass worth of wine in it. I didn't want to find out what boarding an airplane with an open bottle was like, and I was up for a repeat of the previous night's drinking outside with whoever was up for it.

I pulled out my phone and brought up WhatsApp to invite everyone, thinking Emma had my other cracker box and I wanted it back. Then I realized she most likely wouldn't see the message, given how often she didn't bother with the app. She may have been getting ready for bed and I wanted to catch her before she did, so thinking no further, I hurried back to her door, now that I knew which one it was. While I had passed her going into it the night before, I hadn't been paying attention to its location. I knocked, and she opened it, looking tired, even sullen.

"Hey," I began, "sorry to bother you. Did you still want to come out and drink again?"

She considered. "Yeah, I'll come out." Then she shut the door in my face.

I frowned and asked through the door, "Can you bring the cracker box?"

I thought she said yes but wasn't sure and just went back to my room, pouring myself a glass and grabbing my hunk of cheese and the other cracker box. I returned to the veranda, finding Tom out there. He and his Russian girl-friend were a couple that didn't act like one, causing the rest of us to speculate whether they were or were not significant others. Tom was outgoing to her "don't talk to me" vibe that made her unnoticeable. I literally never spoke with her, nor did most of the others, Tom's gregariousness having us talking to him instead.

I said I was waiting for my drinking buddy and asked if he was interested, but he said he and his girlfriend were heading to the bar once she was ready. I said okay and pulled out my phone to invite people, and as I did so, Dot walked past me, announcing she was heading to the bar. I said okay and saw a WhatsApp conversation that I was very late to. Paal was at the bar, inviting people to join him, and everyone who wasn't staying in their rooms was saying yes. I scowled.

I've never been a "bar guy" and hated that one, unable to shake the memory of some weird elderly couple happily dancing and singing antiquated folk tunes on the TV while wearing clothes reminiscent of lederhosen. The bar was long and had two out-of-sync speakers at either end, causing a noticeable delay that I may have been especially irritated by, being a musician. The motel also had that policy plastered everywhere, the one about not drinking what we hadn't bought there. Why pay inflated prices for wine at the bar when I had my own?

Now I stood outside with a full glass. I couldn't have gone to the bar even if I had wanted to because the bartender would have taken one look at me, known she hadn't poured that glass, and made me pour it out, a crime against humanity if ever one existed! If there was a war between Paal at the bar and me outside, I had lost it decisively before even knowing it was being fought.

As I stood there, I saw Darlene and her roommate approaching and hoped to get at least Darlene to hang out with me. Emma emerged with her purse over one shoulder, a bottle of wine discreetly peeking out. She wordlessly handed me the other cracker box at the same moment Darlene and her friend walked past, loudly announcing, "We're headed to the bar!" My invitation died before I even said it. Emma turned to follow them. I watched them go through the glass doors and around the corner, but

Emma stopped to look at a big bug on the wall for far longer than a bug warranted, as if she was waiting for me, but I didn't follow, though I considered it.

I was on a once-in-a-lifetime vacation and while I wasn't a star gazer, I was still here for nature more than culture or anything else, including hanging out with people I had never met before and would never see again, however fun they were. I wanted to sit outside, sip wine, and look at the mountains, maybe play with my star gazing app. If no one was joining me, so be it. And there's an idea that a man in particular should stick to his guns, not be diverted from what he wants by the whims of others. I went back to the room, grabbing my little computer to update my travel log, and then set up shop on one of the wooden chairs with its attached table. I ate cheese and crackers, sipped my wine, and alternated between looking at the scenery and writing. Over the next hour, I slipped into introvert mode, wanting to be myself.

So, when the others suddenly poured out through the glass door, announcing that the bar had closed, I waved off their invitation to join them on the other side of the hedge. That didn't stop someone from sticking their head around the corner and inviting me again a few minutes later. I had already put away the food and empty glass inside, and I now suspected more invitations would make my refusals awkward. Seeing the restaurant's patio in the distance, I moved over there but noticed the more exposed area had the wind hitting me. The temperature had dropped. I was cold. I stood considering whether to deal with it or just go to bed, deciding on the latter, so I headed for the room.

Just after I passed by the opening in the hedge, leading to the lawn where the others were hanging out on the other side, just out of sight, I heard a woman's voice ask incredulously and in disgust, "*Who* did that?"

Emma responded, "Rand."

I stopped in mid-stride, startled. I may have even had one foot still in the air. The unmistakable impression was that Emma was talking shit about me to them. I couldn't believe it, my heart sinking. I stayed where I was, eaves-dropping. Technically, you're not supposed to do that, but then you're not supposed to bad mouth people behind their back either. Sometimes two wrongs do actually make a right. She had done the same thing to Paal the night before. Was it my turn? What on Earth for? What was she saying I had done?

I didn't hear another word for the ten seconds I stood there. This was odd considering that nearly a dozen of them were out there and the chatter had been non-stop. I suspected that someone had seen me walking by the open-ing and whispered that I was right there, pointing at my location, even though they couldn't see me through the thick bushes.

Disturbed, I slipped back to the room, my mood dark-ening. Any interest in Emma had rapidly been doused, and I had apparently done something to kill any interest she might have had. Was it the dolphin swim suggestion? I didn't know and didn't enjoy wondering.

JJ hadn't moved from the bed, still looking at his phone. I sat on the edge of my mattress, which was closer to the rear doors we all used, my back to him.

"Still very disappointed," he remarked.

I wasn't in a joking mood and quietly observed, "Pretty sure Emma has no interest in me." I didn't explain and sat wondering what she was saying to the others. Should I go out there and confront her? Demand an answer so I could defend myself from whatever it was? In that same spot the night before, she had loudly talked about Paal, establishing precedent for making other people look bad without them knowing she was doing it, unable to counter accusations you didn't know were being made.

"Are you okay?" JJ asked, to my surprise. How long had I been sitting there lost in thought? I sensed he thought I was dejected, which was true, but that he might have thought that Emma had rebuffed an advance from me.

With a forced light tone, I said, "Yeah, just thinking." Then I got up and prepared for bed.

Day 6 of 10

The next morning, as I finished packing up, JJ saw that I was already in shoes and asked from where he sat, "Do you mind taking these two bottles back to Adrienne? They're some sort of herbal remedy for my feet. Didn't work and makes a mess."

I shrugged, having heard him complain that the dry skin on his feet was bothering him. "Sure. What room is she in?"

He told me and I went over before she could finish packing up without these. I knocked on the door, which was next to Emma's room, and she opened it, looking surprised to see me. I extended the two bottles, which she took.

"JJ wanted me to give these back to you."

"Okay."

Then I left. We struggled to get breakfast that morning because the motel was supposed to provide it but didn't, leaving JJ exasperated with another screw up. As we stood around for thirty minutes trying to get an answer about all of it, Emma was nowhere to be seen. I went outside to the patio to make room for the others inside, as it was a little crowded, and as I stood there, she came out from another door and approached me while I stood taking a photo of the mountains.

"It's so pretty here," she said, stopping and looking at what I was photographing.

I looked sideways at her. I have never been one for playing dumb, but that didn't mean I was going to admit I knew about the night before. I just didn't care to pretend it hadn't happened. I would not be friendly to her. All I said, without enthusiasm, was, "Yeah."

Then I walked away.

We all got breakfast in town before boarding the bus back to Christchurch, where we briefly met the tour guide for the last time, as she apologized for the mistakes and assured us there would be no more; she was right. Then we boarded the flight to Queenstown, which bills itself as the Adventure Capital of the World. This was the only location where we had no group activities, each of us on our own to book something, but my excitement rose because we were now headed straight into the beautiful landscape for which I had come.

During this day to get there, I kept my distance from Emma, not trusting her and noticing that she also seemed to avoid not only me, but many in the group, being uncharacteristically quiet, especially for someone so talkative and who loved attention. While waiting to pick up our luggage in Queenstown, she stood off to one side alone, eyes down and faraway, looking depressed. I wondered if something had happened but would not ask. She remained that way as we boarded our new bus for the rest of the trip, a trailer on the back carrying the luggage.

That's when we met Kent, the driver. He was my age or older, balding, laid-back, rugged, and masculine. He was funny and had a great memory for names. Raised north of Christchurch but living in Queenstown, he used to do tours like this for a living but worked as a gardener now, only doing tours when he didn't have custody of his 11-year-old daughter. We all liked him far more than our previous driver, especially when Adrienne and a few others tried to jokingly sass mouth him and he zinged them back even better.

Emma and I continued to subtly avoid each other, not sitting near on the bus or for a meal, never standing by the other, and engaging in no chitchat beyond a second or two, with me always stepping away from her when it happened. I scrutinized the others for signs of a change in attitude toward me based on whatever Emma had been saying about me, but I saw nothing and shrugged it off. I just didn't want Emma around me, and with the lack of pre-planned activities, mostly got my wish.

One opportunity in town was a luge ride, the name falsely suggesting it was like the winter sport. To one side of town was a small mountain. A ski lift takes riders to the top, where you walk across concrete to the starting area, where single-person karts await. They have little more than brake pedals and a steering wheel, because gravity pulls you down the concrete track with its twists and turns, and the occasional small hill for a speed boost. Most of it is wide enough to pass slower riders until the end, when you are funneled into a narrow path to the finish, where you disembark. From there, you can board the lift again or leave if your pre-purchased ticket count is up.

A handful in our group had already gone to the place when more of us decided to, rushing to walk across town to it before they closed. Once we got tickets, somehow JJ, Paal, and I found ourselves together throughout, acting like little boys because we bought a package of six tickets each and had to rush to use them before closing. The result was hurtling down as fast as possible, racing each other. Then at the bottom we literally ran to the ski lift, and once off it at the top, we again ran like little kids to the start and went down ASAP.

During it all, I was videotaping with a GoPro in one hand because my head mount wasn't working, adding to the challenge of steering. One time, I made it on the lift on the bottom without them, riding up alone. At the top, as I walked to let them catch up, I encountered Emma by herself, leaning against a railing with an overlook of the track's top. She saw me coming, and to my surprise, smiled.

"How was it?" she asked, not sounding interested in the answer. This didn't surprise me.

Figure 10 The Luge in Queenstown

I answered as I neared, not stopping. "It's good. You aren't doing it?"

"No, not a good idea with my ankle."

"I think you'd be fine." I passed her and looked back, seeing JJ and Paal getting off the lift and running toward us. She heard them coming and turned to them.

"Oh my God, you guys! How is it? It looks like so much fun!" The loud, over-the-top enthusiasm that she used to ask them the same question as me struck me and I almost laughed. I sensed and felt that this was a passive-aggressive message to me, as I was clearly within earshot of her hollering. And that message was that I was disfavored. Bothered by the attempt at assigning me inferior status, and not understanding what had changed since Kaikoura, I tried to shrug it off and resumed the luge.

We got all but one of our rides in, and the group, which included about a dozen of us, departed for town on foot, trying to find somewhere for dinner. From the luge, I enjoyed the view of the lake and mountains, but I felt surprised at the lack of snow on them, mostly due to the season. I thought the peaks would have been higher, so some disappointment muted my appreciation. Now as we walked through town for the second time, I had more time to look around; the first time, we'd been in a hurry to reach the luge.

Queenstown's atmosphere reminded me of a modern metropolis on a smaller scale, the buildings and signs refurbished or new. Maybe the downtown area was indeed fresh. It had an inviting quality that made me want to stay. Having no car and needing to walk around suited me. Most of the buildings were only two or three stories, the sidewalks were clean, and people were everywhere but not in such high numbers as to feel crowded. I already wanted to return for longer than we had.

When we learned there was a very popular burger joint named Fergburger, where a line went down the street to get inside, Emma returned to an old behavior. "Eating a fur burger" is slang for performing cunnilingus on a woman who hasn't shaved. And while the rest of us humored her, Emma began a string of comments.

"Ah, that's so funny! I really want to eat a fergburger!"

"I came to New Zealand just to eat a fergburger!"

"I'm gonna tell all my friends I ate a fergburger in Queenstown!"

"Look at all these people desperate for a fergburger!"

While I didn't spend time near her much anymore, and the stimulus of seeing Groper Garage had passed, I now realized she hadn't said she wanted to be groped since I warned her to quit it. But now she had a new joke she wouldn't stop making at every opportunity. I belatedly realized she was just immature, like a stereotypical teenage boy. I once again exchanged looks with others in the group as we rolled our eyes a bit, mostly because Emma was once again overdoing it. We ended up at an outdoor Asian restaurant, where I purposely sat away from her and busied myself with other friends and watching the darkness descend, the lights of Queenstown coming on one by one. This was already my favorite place.

Day 7 of 10

The next day, I was on my own, having struggled to decide on which adventures to do. I settled on a high-speed boat ride over the lake, where the driver would do a sudden 180 spin as water splashed over us. Then he took us along a river to a drop off point. We exited, already wearing wetsuits, and got into two different rafts. The river's calmness occasionally gave way to mild whitewater rapids, where I caught the brunt of it in the front, but it was outstanding. Our skipper told us to jump out at one point and we floated down the chilly waters, only my face and hands feeling it.

Getting back in the raft was easy with a tug from a peer, and we eventually got out again, this time to climb a cliff. Most of us were brave enough to make the resulting leap back into the river from at least thirty feet up—just far enough that I really felt myself falling. But no sooner did that feeling strike than I had to prepare to strike the water with considerable force, made a little worse by my life vest creating more resistance. The river had been used to film *The Lord of the Rings*, the sequence where they approach two giant statues with their hands outstretched. But it looked nothing like that, significant CGI altering it, so this was hugely disappointing.

My companies were strangers, many from nearby Australia, but they were an excellent group and we all laughed a lot along the way. One local told a memorable joke— what's the difference between a petri dish and New Zealand? After a thousand years, the petri dish will develop some culture. This appeared to be a joke Australians tell about their smaller neighbor, but no one seemed to mind it.

After cleaning up, I rode the event bus back to town, and as I got off, I found Adam the virgin and Emma on the street corner talking.

"Hey guys," I casually said, approaching. I was in a good mood and feeling friendly, even toward Emma, as I shrugged off her weird vibes.

"Hey," Emma curtly replied with a half-glance before returning to Adam, who she was still talking to, hardly giving him a chance to greet me. He settled for nodding at me. Emma's demeanor brought me up short, forcibly reminding me of the silent attitude from her. She talked to Adam for a minute before hugging him and walking away as if I didn't exist.

Okay, I thought, *now I know something is going on.* While we had avoided each other since the last morning in Kaikoura, this had been subtle by both of us. If chance had brought us together, I had pretended to be normal, mostly, and so had she, but I had still been wondering if something was going on that I didn't know about. The weirdness at the luge had been the first minor attitude, but this had a "fuck off" vibe to it. I now felt the same and would privately celebrate her every absence from group activities. I don't like stuff like this. It is childish.

I talked to Adam for a minute before parting ways, but I later saw him at the hotel. I entered through the front door and walked around the corner, nearly running into Roz, who was trying to get into her room, so now I knew hers was the first off the lobby, not that I cared. As I walked down the long hall, Adam stood at the other end, his left side turned slightly toward me, an exit door behind him. I wondered why he was standing there so long, looking distracted, but he finally pulled out a room key that he had apparently been fishing for in a pocket and let himself in to his room right there. I now knew where his room was. Adrienne's room was across from mine with JJ, which I knew from seeing her come and go at the same time as me. The reason I mention these will become apparent.

Most of us agreed to meet and party that night in a big suite that Tom and his girlfriend had been given. We pooled our various wines, my crackers and giant hunk of cheese, and fruits someone bought. Emma and the Asian women didn't show up, to my relief, having gone searching for dive bars.

I hung out with Paal, and the talk somehow turned to Emma's comments about him making her uncomfortable. Apparently, word had gotten to him. He admitted to the line about hitting on her if he was ten years younger but said he only made the remark once, not three times. He seemed genuine, apologetic, and embarrassed about the whole thing. I believed him and made a point of telling him so, because I could tell that he knew someone had bad-mouthed him and I wanted him *not* to think everyone thought little of him.

That I was dimly aware the same might have been done to me didn't really affect this, because I could only speculate what Emma had said about me. And I had nothing. No one had breathed a word of it to me, and I wondered why. But I had been on the receiving end of very malicious gossip in my teens and twenties, rumors that had literally destroyed my life and caused ostracism, isolation, and severe depression. I automatically feel sympathy for anyone treated this way. Any remaining esteem in which I held Emma vaporized on seeing Paal's muted distress and desire to acquit himself to someone, which happened to be me. So I gave it to him. One person, at least, would respect him, and give him the benefit of the doubt.

Figure 11 Near Queenstown

We became friendlier starting that night.

I tend to be reasonable and almost overly interested in fairness, qualities that I have suspected are apparent, and if someone is looking for a kind ear, they can find it in me. I assume the best of others, not go with an assumption of guilt, and I had little doubt Paal sensed it and appreciated my response, even if I still had some doubts about who was telling the truth; I kept those to myself. Still, I had seen him keeping his distance from Emma, and JJ and I had talked about him apparently having gotten the message, which he respected enough to avoid Emma. That told me a lot right there, and I felt he had integrity. Emma? Not so much.

Day 8 of 10

The next day, we had time for one last early morning excursion in Queenstown, with me, JJ, and the other Asian guy going on another high-speed river event where the boat did sudden 180 degree turns at full speed. We returned, cleaned up, and checked out of the Queenstown hotel with everyone else, boarding the bus for a pit stop in Arrowtown, an historic mining town. This wasn't part of our planned activities, but our bus driver Kent thought we could squeeze it in. We wandered around a street or two of old, picturesque buildings and little shops, some of us eating ice cream. I ran across two buskers playing beautiful, haunting music on Chapman Sticks, a guitar-like instrument, the sound permeating the air. This added to the pleasant atmosphere, and I chatted with them a while before buying a CD. I had wondered about this place and appreciated getting to see it after all.

We then boarded the bus for the long ride through plains and adjacent mountains to Te Anau, a rural town of two-story buildings and a postcard-worthy lake. We saw little of the town, which reminded me of a big neighborhood. If attractions existed away from the lake, we weren't seeing them, but the pleasant vibe made it seem like a good place to relax. I would not have the chance to experience this, for the dark whisperer in my midst was about to strike.

When we arrived and exited the bus at our motel, a woman named Monica met us outside as Kent unloaded the luggage. Monica revealed that she had printed a piece of paper with everyone's names and room numbers on it, leaving a copy in each room. When JJ saw the copy she handed him in the parking lot as we all stood there, he reacted badly. He went by his initials, but she had printed his full name. He was very upset and said he didn't want anyone knowing his actual name. Realizing that she had inadvertently offended the group host, Monica was unhappy.

"I thought everyone would want to know where everyone's room was," she said, sounding confused and concerned. "This way you know where to find each other. I always do this."

"Yeah," started JJ, "but I don't want my actual name on them. Can you change this, please? Reprint them? I'll go collect them from every room."

"Sure. Sure. Whatever you want. I'm sorry."

"It's okay," he said, though it clearly wasn't. "Can you let me into every room so I can get them?"

"Sure."

We all stood watching this, some of us exchanging a raised eyebrow. The room I shared with him was right in front of us, and he went in with me to confiscate the paper before I saw it, so I asked about this after dragging my luggage inside.

"Just curious why this matters so much to you? No offense meant."

"I just really hate my first name," he said, sounding distressed. "And I have like forty thousand people in this group and the other. The last thing I need is people friending me on Facebook or LinkedIn and shit. I learned that the hard way."

"Makes sense." Now I was dying to know what his first name was.

He left to grab the other copies as I put my bags out of the way. I knew we only had a few minutes because we were due to hop on the bus for a five-minute drive to the lake where we would board a sightseeing boat to "glow worm caves." This did not terribly excite me, because they were worms, even if they glowed, but it was something to see anyway. After a minute, I heard JJ come down the stairs from the second floor and encounter Monica again.

"You know what?" he began. "Forgot about the sheets."

"You don't want them? It's no problem."

"No, one of the women said she was very uncomfortable when one guy knocked on her room at another hotel, because he knew her room number."

"Oh, okay."

Overhearing this brought me up short. I knew at once that the woman was Emma, and the guy was me. My startled reaction turned to sobering disbelief at the obvious implication—the reason a woman would feel uncomfortable was fear that the man would sexually assault her. My jaw hit the floor.

Wait. What? Holy shit. Is she serious?

I had been on the receiving end of unwanted sexually contact several times, by both guys and a woman, and would never do it to someone. It causes fury, indignation, adrenaline, and fear or worse to come. It also instantly turns someone against you, to put it mildly, and causing that reaction to me wasn't something I did except by accident, and while I had my moments of stupidity, not realizing this impact of assault wasn't one of them.

I was beyond astonished that she feared this from me. How could she think that? She couldn't be serious. But then a kaleidoscope of images for nearly everything that had happened since Kaikoura flashed through my head, my mind settling on the image of her at the Queenstown airport the next day, standing apart from everyone, eyes faraway, an air of apprehension and muted turmoil about her. It sobered me even more. She believed it.

Oh my God.

JJ entered the room with his bags, and I turned away, struggling to process this and not wanting to interact.

I had never complimented Emma, never expressed admiration, never overtly flirted. I had been nothing other than polite, a gentleman. I had even warned her not to keep saying she wanted someone to grope her so that someone else would not assault her. How could she believe I wanted to do it? I was appalled and felt terrible for this misunderstanding, but there wasn't a trace of guilt in me, just empathy and compassion. She had spent several days in a group around me while worrying about this all the time? It was horrible for her. I had to let her know that this simply wasn't an option, that there was no reason to fear this, and do it immediately.

But knocking on her door to do so was obviously out of the question, and as usual, I had no idea which room she was in anyway. Having this conversation in person likely meant others overhearing it, an idea that made me cringe. The only remaining option was WhatsApp, though she probably wouldn't see the message for a while. Without thinking it through, I pulled out my phone and began typing.

This was unfamiliar territory for me, and I wasn't sure what to say. I just wanted her to go back to being comfortable, to not feel unsafe, to not feel a cloud of fear over her head. I dropped my guard to impart my sincerity as I sent her an apology, which I did not believe I owed her because I was certain I had not genuinely done anything wrong, but I wanted to apologize anyway as a sign of good faith. And I *was* genuinely remorseful that this had somehow happened, though I didn't understand it at all. Here is what I wrote:

Emma,

I'm so sorry.

I heard JJ tell the owner that someone didn't want room numbers known because someone unexpectedly knocked on her door and made her uncomfortable. I knew who was meant by this. I've been aware of your avoidance of me since I knocked on your door the other day and have wondered if I'd somehow upset you. That you'd feel uncomfortable was absolutely not intentional.

I always want women to feel comfortable with me and feel terrible that I did the opposite. I am more the sort to step in and help women. I would like nothing more than for you to go back to being comfortable. I sense that this can't happen with me around, so I will continue to remain apart from you from now on, keeping my distance.

Rand

I wasn't sure what else to say and was so focused on what I wrote that I never thought about the reaction until it showed up minutes later, the speed making it clear she fired it off at once.

Um yeah so when no one knew each other's room numbers (I didn't know yours or anyone else's who wasn't immediately next to me from running into them in the hallway) and you knock on my door letting me know you were somehow taking notes on where I was sleeping, that is CREEPY.

You are what, 15-20 years older than me? Knocking on my door and asking me to come drink with you away from the group is extremely creepy.

This message is even creepier.

Before that, trying to get me to have dinner alone with you and telling me I can't make jokes about the groper or you're going to "show me what it's like" to get groped is fucking creepy. I should have told you to fuck off but just tried to laugh it off and ignore it to not make this trip awkward as fuck.

I try to be nice and friendly with everyone. I know men sometimes misread that, but your behavior has made me extremely uncomfortable. This message is totally bizarre. Really don't give a shit if you think you are some kind of protector of women, whatever the fuck that means. Texting me "I want us apart" is creepy. I can protect myself from creepos like you and have been doing so for a long time.

Thank you for making me throw up in my mouth. Please leave me alone. Thx.

There are times when you instantly sense great hostility toward you from the first moments of something and a wall flies up inside you, but sometimes it just isn't fast enough because you are caught so off guard. I felt beyond floored. My guard was down and every blow she fired at me struck home. I couldn't keep up with her bizarre logic, the conclusion jumping, the name calling, the ageism, the mischaracterizations, the self-exoneration, the vilification, the self-satisfied smugness and pride, the condescension, the outright lying, and the sheer backwardness of it all. She cast innocent actions of mine as over-the-top creepiness that warranted a threat of violence against me. Confusion and a surging desire to get away from the blatant hostility dominated my emotional reaction. If anyone had been watching my face, I would assume the color had drained from it as I stared in silent shock at my phone.

And then suddenly I remembered the moment in Kaikoura when I had walked past the hedge to return to my room and heard someone ask in disbelieving disgust, "Who did that?" And Emma's response, "Rand."

Waves of humiliation and shame crashed over me, adrenaline making my chest, arms, or legs shake at random, my clothes instantly damp with perspiration, heat rising in my chest and face. This was what she had been telling them. For three days now. That I was stalking her. That I threatened to grope her. That I tried to get her to go off to dinner alone and drink alone with me so I could get her drunk and rape her.

Who had she told this to? Who had believed it? How many of them had been pretending to be civil to my face while believing these horrendous lies about me? For three days! And all the while, I did not know. Were they laughing at me? Badmouthing me like some had done to Paal? Evaluating, judging, watching to see if it was all true, that I was a groping, stalking, rapist?

I stood frozen to the spot, JJ having gone outside to join the others as a rapidly thickening, protective wall gathered around me. I fumbled with the phone, instinctively rejecting it all by typing, "This is nuts." I hit send and was going to try clearing up some of the utter deceit hurled at me, though I had no idea where to begin, but I lost my connection in the very rural area we were in. When I got it back a minute later, there was a last message from Emma.

LOL you're gross. And blocked! Thx!

I immediately blocked her as well, desperate to turn off the tidal wave of scorn, hate, amusement, and sheer nastiness coming at me over WhatsApp. I had never been called "gross" before, a deeply insulting thing to say to a man, and which conjured images of an unkempt, uneducated slob picking his nose and eating it. I had never been called a creep, not to mention so many times. And I deserved to be blocked? For giving a heartfelt, conscientious apology to someone who hadn't even deserved it.

JJ called my name because the bus was getting ready to leave. I stood unmoving with indecision. I wanted nothing to do with any of them. It was too soon, a black cloud of awful suspicion awaiting me outside that room. I couldn't process anything, make sense of it. A deep anger lurked somewhere inside but didn't come out, or couldn't, as if I was so confused that it didn't know where to go and just randomly made parts of my body shake. I felt dazed, my head in a fog, like I was somehow disconnected from my trembling body. I almost wondered what was going on with me, but I knew.

I was in psychological shock.

JJ and a few others called again, and I felt myself slowly moving toward the door, putting on my sunglasses to hide my eyes as I exited. I felt afraid that once among them, without warning, another unwarranted attack on me would erupt, this time from someone else. Now that Emma had told me the accusations she had been making, were the others free to chime in at me, adding the weight of consensus to their damnation? Had she just told everyone, "Yeah, I told him off now," freeing them to say something, too? Maybe it was paranoia, but I knew for a fact that she had badmouthed Paal, and me.

I was the last to board the bus, eyes immediately searching for Emma to avoid her, but she sat in the middle, and the front had too many people. She was gaily chatting with someone and laughing as if she hadn't just sent this nasty message. Or maybe they were talking about that very thing, joking and bonding about sticking it to the gross creep. Was she gloating? Celebrating?

I went past her and found a place in the back to sit alone, avoiding interaction. My timing had resulted in others already being in conversation and no one bothering with me. The trip was a few minutes. I exited the bus last, keeping my distance, acutely uncomfortable and trailing along by five to ten feet behind the nearest group member. We had arrived at a boathouse with souvenirs around us, waiting for the two-deck ferry we would board in minutes.

I continued staying away from them, but Paal stopped beside me, facing the same direction as the lake.

"Are you okay?" he asked, to my surprise.

When we're not okay and someone asks us this, there's a tendency to say yes anyway. I don't know why most of us do this, but it's a known phenomenon. We could almost lay there with a severed artery pumping our life's blood onto the ground and still say yes to this. But I was still so stunned and mute that I only turned to him and slowly shook my head. I was not alright. I was not normal. And it upset me enough that I had no energy to pretend otherwise, to play along. I couldn't encourage this conversation for fear of what he might say about Emma's rumoring. At that moment, I wasn't thinking about him being on the receiving end of it, too, and he might be the last one to believe it. This didn't even occur to me, but then I couldn't think straight.

Before he could respond, someone on his other side said something to him and when he looked at them, I turned away, moving past multiple souvenir stands to create distance between us, warding off any further questions. We soon left the building for the long dock, me again trailing behind at a distance designed to create plausible deniability that I was doing it on purpose. Normally, when you're with a group and see it leaving, you hurry to catch up to avoid being left behind. But I was doing the opposite, purposely making sure every last person had already gone and was ten feet ahead before I followed. I hadn't spoken since the hotel. I had lost all interest in the beautiful lake, the surrounding mountains, or the cave destination.

On the two-level sightseeing boat, as others entered the bottom and mingled, I immediately climbed a staircase to the top to be alone, but others soon came up. They went to the front, so I moved to the back, alone against the white metal railing, facing them only so I could see if someone was approaching and leave before they reached me. At some point I felt too many people were up there, including Emma, and I went down again to keep away. After a while, Adrienne approached me, putting a hand on my arm.

"Is everything okay? I kind of feel like it's not."

For a moment I wondered how she could tell, but it had to be obvious. I imagine I had a defensive, tightly coiled, "leave me alone" posture and a flat, mask-like expression that had replaced my casual, laid-back demeanor, any gregariousness and joking, and my approachability. The contrast was likely stark but would have been familiar to anyone who knew me as a deeply distressed and depressed child, teenager, or young adult. Emma had hurled me into a darkness I had not felt in two decades.

I wordlessly shook my head again.

"Okay, well if you want to talk, any time. I know it always helps me."

I sincerely appreciated that, partly from my distress, but also from a lifetime of being on my own to deal with such things. I forced myself to respond, "Thank you. That means a lot to me. I just can't now."

"Sure. Whenever you are, let me know."

"*Thank* you."

She took the hint and left me alone. Part of me felt bad not taking her up on the offer, but I didn't know if she was one of the people who'd been told these lies. I trusted no one.

At our destination, we listened to a guide, boarded a canoe or rowboat, and silently floated through dark caverns with little white or blue pinpricks of light dotting the ceiling. These were the glow worms we had come to see. Afterward, we watched a presentation and had hot chocolate, then went outside for a few minutes of walking around on multiple boardwalks that led through the trees to the lake shore twenty-five yards from the building. During it all, I studiously avoided everyone, sitting away from them among strangers who didn't know of my groping, stalking, rapist reputation. I planned my avoidance by always trailing along behind, seeing my opportunities, and taking them. I wasn't enjoying any of it, partly because it wasn't that interesting anyway, but I was too distracted to care.

For example, I stayed next to the building as everyone else went to the shoreline. Seeing them returning, I sensed that someone might talk to me if I remained there when they reached me, so I approached them, not to join them, but to pass them. There would be no chance to speak for more than a second. It worked each time until the final boardwalk. As I reached the shore and the others were most of the way back, Darlene was straggling. From behind me, she let the others continue without her.

"Hey Rand," she said, her tone conciliatory. Recognizing her voice, I reluctantly turned around to see her ten paces from me, wearing an expression of concern with a kind of feigned hopefulness overlaid on it. "Are you okay?"

For the third time, I shook my head at the question.

Smiling as if to ingratiate herself with me, Darlene said, "Do you want to talk about it? I'm a good listener."

I again forced myself to express my gratitude. "I would love to, and I really appreciate you saying that. I...I just need time to think."

"Okay. No worries. I kind of knew something was up. I have a sense about these things from having five brothers. Guys let on in their own way."

I nodded. She was probably hard to hide things from anyway, not that I was trying to. She left, and we soon boarded the boat back, me once again staying off the same level as most of the group, and consistently choosing a side where no one was, even being obvious about avoiding them if people came near me and I moved away. Let them notice. I would rather have them talk about that than whether I was planning an assault on Emma, or say something to me about the creepiness therein, confirming they believed her.

At some point, Adrienne came around a corner to find me leaning against a bulkhead alone, arms crossed. She held out her arms, wearing a smiling expression that somewhat jokingly said, "Can I help? Do you want a hug?" I forced a slight smirk, still hiding behind my sunglasses, but she gave me the hug anyway, me not returning it, before she walked away.

Once at the dock, I again trailed them into and out of the boathouse, which stood at a T-intersection. Straight ahead was the road we'd used to arrive before, restaurants lining both sides. To the left and right ran a lakeside road with low buildings on the opposite side. They seemed mostly like housing.

As the group talked about where to get dinner, the light to cross the street changed for them and they marched across. I did not, looking to my left, seeing a path along the lake. I sped that way, repeatedly glancing back to see if anyone noticed me fleeing as they crossed the road and headed down the sidewalk. We were close enough that we could walk back to the hotel, but I made my escape in the opposite direction. And when they and I had gone far enough, with no chance of anyone seeing me anymore, I slowed. I had finally escaped from them and the cloud of suspicion. The fog in my head cleared, the cool air as night that descended almost helping, like cold water splashed in my face. I found a bench and sat down. I badly needed my normal, calm, logical demeanor to return, so I first spent ten minutes spacing out.

Then I began to think, the surrounding landscape forgotten even though it was the reason I was there.

I wanted a mental review of everything that had happened with me and Emma, partly to understand what I could have done to inspire the accusations. I was sure of my innocence, but I needed to banish the blame she had put inside me. That was first. Figuring out where she had gotten this stuff from could come later. I didn't have a plan, but I thought things through while there for a half hour, then got dinner alone, walking past the boat house and down the other way along the lake until I found a burger joint with a pool table and live music that was still setting up. And I kept thinking, eating alone and ignoring my surroundings.

When I left, I tried to continue down that road, knowing the hotel was down there somewhere but back a block or two from the street, but each time I tried to cut through the parking lot of a building, it was only to find a tall wall or unclimbable fence.

I conceded defeat and returned to the T-intersection, reluctantly walking in the direction the group had gone, not wanting to run into them. There was a 50-50 chance they were eating at the side of the street I was on, another 50-50 chance that they were doing so outside on the very wide decks that were only a couple feet high and at nearly each eatery. With any luck, their tables would be up against the building, not right by the sidewalk.

After passing several places, eyes scanning for signs of them, I saw them on my side of the street (shit!), outside (shit!), by the building (whew!), at least thirty feet away, empty tables separating us. I turned my head away and pretended to be fascinated by something in the distance. And then I heard multiple women crying out my name, inviting me over, but I kept going. I took some solace in this, figuring no one had a fetish for groping, stalking, rapist dinner guests, and maybe some of them didn't believe any of it. Certainly, Darlene and Adrienne hadn't appeared to. I didn't know what to think and was just exhausted.

I found the hotel and opened my diary, looking forward to working out more of my mental review in solitude, but JJ arrived minutes later, as everyone was retiring for the night. He asked if I had heard them calling my name, but I lied and said no. Fortunately, he went to sleep soon enough.

I continued my mental run through to try making sense of Emma's rant.

The first supposed incident between Emma and I in Kaikoura had been when I asked her if she still wanted to go eat sushi. Or maybe it was when I asked her to visit Groper Garage. She had not specified which suggestion made me a creep.

Starting with the sushi place, she claimed I wanted her to go off alone with me for this, but I never said that. I had made the sushi suggestion to the group at least twice that day. Why did she think it was only for her now? Just because she was the only one standing there? This is reasonable, but it was a coincidence. She happened to be the first of the three women to exit the store they were shopping in, stepping out just as I returned. I told her at once due to urgency, not to whisk her away before the others came out. Any sensible person knows that a restaurant that is closing in thirty minutes doesn't leave a lot of time to get there, order, and eat.

When she suggested learning what the others wanted to do, I immediately agreed because that was my intention as well. I had not re-invited the others yet because they were still inside. Given that I had made the suggestion to the entire group several times, the assumption likely should have been that anyone who wanted to come was welcome. Emma assuming otherwise was her mistake, and calling me a creep was inappropriate. In reality, I was being polite. I had scoped out the place, hurried back, and then confirmed if she was still interested rather than ditching her and the others and doing it without them. Each had previously expressed interest and yet likely knew no more than I had that the place was about to close. Until I told them.

After we ditched the sushi place, Emma and I were once again standing alone on the street. I suggested Groper Garage and this time, I explicitly said out loud that I knew people in our group had been discussing eating there. The clear implication was to join them, assuming they were indeed there; that there was some risk they would not be is important because Emma went there with me anyway, so even if she thought *this* was to be just us, she condoned it. She continued with me even after the Asian women rejoined us and then peeled off to eat somewhere else.

And if this invite was explicitly to join others in the group, why would she assume the previous sushi invite was only for her? Because I did not explicitly state otherwise that time? It's the only difference between the two. If one invite was explicit and the other ambiguous, doesn't hindsight suggest both were like the explicit invitation, especially given that I offered no resistance to others joining us when *she* explicitly said it?

But let's say for the sake of argument that she was right, and I had wanted dinner to be just the two of us. Why would that make me a creep? People do this literally every day. By her rationale, all people who ask someone to eat with them are creeps and should be told so. The restaurant business better hope this idea doesn't catch on because they would all go out of business. There is also nothing creepy about a guy asking a woman if she *still* wants to go to dinner after she has *repeatedly* said she wanted to. And given all the times she had suggested I grope her (which, by the way, is creepy), might I not have been excused for thinking she would welcome some time alone with me and my supposedly roving hands? *This* is the sort of "creepy" behavior that she was inviting with her groping suggestions, and which *I* told her to stop inviting!

Before that, trying to get me to have dinner alone with you and telling me I can't make jokes about the groper or you're going to "show me what it's like" to get groped is fucking creepy. I should have told you to fuck off but just tried to laugh it off and ignore it to not make this trip awkward as fuck.

And groping was the second supposed incident between us. Her comments about it suggested a double-standard. It was okay for her to say nearly two dozen times that she wanted to be groped, but wrong of me to tell her once to stop it before someone did it? She missed the obvious, unambiguous intent of my words. She was literally encouraging people to grope her, and their lack of desire to do so, or their superior sense of it being inappropriate, was stopping them. Say it in front of the wrong person, such as those two guys who wanted her bra, and she would set herself up for the resulting sexual assault. I wanted her to stop inviting this both for her own sake and because it made me uncomfortable. How did that make me a creep?

It was true that I had not added, "I do not mean that *I* am going to grope you." At worst, this is an oversight. It never occurred to me that she would interpret it that way. I don't know how gropers operate, but in retrospect, I likely assumed they don't typically announce their intentions ahead of time and therefore I would not be mistaken for someone intending to grope her. I deserved the benefit of the doubt, especially given how many times she had already said it and I had not taken her up on the suggestion.

Even if I had said or meant what she claimed, that I was going to grope her if she said it again, isn't that exactly what she kept telling me she wanted someone to do, often while looking at me? How can she be offended if I were to essentially say, "Okay, I'll do it?" I assumed she was not serious—that was part of my warning, that if she kept saying it, someone might think she was. Why would she assume I would be serious...unless she had been serious? And if that were true, then in theory she would be pleased that I finally groped her.

She was also suggesting I had threatened to do it, but that implies it is unwelcome when she was repeatedly inviting it. If she really thought that I had just threatened to grope her, then why did she walk down the street with me, turn down a chance to ditch me at the Indian restaurant, and sit next to me at the now infamous Groper Garage when she could have gone or sat elsewhere? It doesn't add up, and I was increasingly certain I had done nothing wrong.

I will also admit that this was unfamiliar territory for me, having a woman repeatedly say she wants to be groped. Should I get some slack for not being sure what to say to make her quit it without bothering her when I did? If we don't make other people uncomfortable with weird behavior, then maybe they won't have a response that makes us feel just as uncomfortable. She claims she didn't punch me to avoid making "the trip awkward as fuck." Too late.

While Emma may not have meant the groping comments literally, she could still have been flirting with me by making them to me so often. When I told her to knock it off, she may have seen that as rejection. This would explain her going quiet for a minute but also continuing down the street with me and eating dinner beside me, as if she was brushing it off and trying to determine if I still had any interest by spending more time with me to judge that. Later that night, when I didn't follow her inside to drink with the others, I chose the New Zealand countryside over her. Was she a woman scorned?

The third incident was about knocking on her door and asking if she still wanted to come out and drink again.

Um yeah so when no one knew each other's room numbers (I didn't know yours or anyone else's who wasn't immediately next to me from running into them in the hallway) and you knock on my door letting me know you were somehow taking notes on where I was sleeping, that is CREEPY.

You are what, 15-20 years older than me? Knocking on my door and asking me to come drink with you away from the group is extremely creepy.

She suggests that the true reason I knocked on her door was to let her know that I was "somehow" keeping tabs on where she was sleeping. This suggests an unknown, sinister, underhanded move by my cunning self. And yet, in the same sentence, she acknowledges the exact way by which I can come to know—seeing people entering or exiting their room. She simultaneously acknowledged that this was ordinary and yet suggested that the only reason *I* could know where *her* room lay was that I had been stalking her.

I only knew her room location once out of four hotels/motels, because she and Paal were entering their adjacent rooms at the same time, and she had said he was making her uncomfortable. And Paal's room was the first after the lobby. It doesn't take a genius to remember that hers was the second one, especially for the next five minutes. Having rudimentary observations skills doesn't make you a stalker.

I knew no one else's room location at the first and final hotels because of *my* room's location. I knew where Darlene's room was once because she wanted me to kill two spiders there. I knew where Roz's room was in Queenstown because I almost ran into her while she was entering it. Something similar happened there with Adam, then Adrienne twice—first when JJ had me knock on her door to return the herbal remedies for his feet, and again when her room was across from ours in Queenstown. JJ had sent me to Adrienne's room the first time. Had Adrienne thought I was stalking her? Had JJ known one of us would get that reaction and so he sent me, the dick? Of course not.

Emma specifically said I knocked on her door to let her know that I not only knew where she was sleeping, but that I wanted her to know that I knew. And that I would continue to take notes on this from now on? This also suggested she could not stop me, since she couldn't stop me without figuring out how I was achieving this feat, leaving her perpetually vulnerable to my impending assault. She cast e asking her to come drink again as my excuse for doing this via knocking, providing me plausible deniability—I was purposely instilling this fear but could pretend that this was not what I was really doing. The invitation to drink was a ruse. This is extreme paranoia.

It also makes little sense. If that was how she felt when I knocked, then why did she agree to come out, do so, and bring a bottle of wine? The obvious answer is that this is not how she felt at the time. Because none of it was true, and she knew better. So why was she saying it? I wasn't sure yet.

Emma used the phrase "where I was sleeping," revealing her sense of vulnerability. It suggested I would wait until after midnight to pick the lock and then assault her. If I had made a note of her room to assault her inside late at night, then why did I invite her *outside* to drink hours earlier? Shouldn't I have invited myself in when I knocked? It makes little sense. And where was that sense of vulnerability all those times she said she wanted to be groped? She was hardly some innocent victim in all of this. Something had changed to make her go from making the groping comments to feeling so uncomfortable—and this happened *after* our last interaction in Kaikoura, after she went inside to the bar and I remained outside to drink alone—by my decision. Given that we were not around each other after that, how could I be responsible for the change from *grope me* and *yeah I'll come out and drink with you*, to "you're a creep?"

In Te Anau where we still were, the *female* innkeeper had printed everyone's names and room numbers and put a copy in everyone's room. Was she trying to make it easier for the guys to creep out the women? Obviously not. It had been a courtesy so that we knew where to find each other and *knock on their door*. Even a *woman* who ran a tourist hotel thought it was okay to make sure a group of guests knew this info. And no one else objected. Didn't this suggest that this knowledge was not typically nefarious, and I should be given the benefit of the doubt that me having it (once) did not mean something sinister?

The intent she assigned me was fictional. There were no actions that suggested I intended any of what she projected onto me. I never broke into her room. I didn't barge in. I didn't ask if I could come inside. I had knocked, which is an act of politeness. And when she opened the door, I had stayed right where I was. I made no compliments, no innuendo, no banter even. I invited her out. Another act of politeness. While I wanted my cracker box back, I was also making sure she knew of this get together instead of letting her get left out because she seldom used WhatsApp and wouldn't see that invite. Something is very wrong when acting like a gentleman gets you viewed as a stalker.

I had asked if she *still* wanted to come out. Why? She had previously expressed an interest in repeating what we had already done the night before. And that had included other people. Both established precedent—she had said yes before, and we had done it before, and she had admitted wanting to repeat it. Therefore, me inviting and confirming she still wanted to was appropriate, even expected.

While I did not specifically mention other people, I also did not specifically say it was just going to be me and her. The implication should have been that others would be there *again*. And the physical circumstances (sitting within earshot of rooms) made it highly likely that others would realize we were there and join us, even if we did not invite them. Because that was exactly what had happened the night before.

And how much difference was there between asking her the night before while she was stepping into her room, and asking her the same question the next night after knocking on the already closed door? In one case, I happened to be walking by. In the other, I had returned to knock. One was fine, but the other meant I was a stalking creep who wanted to rape her? And yet, for the second time, she said yes. And she didn't say it just to get rid of me and then not come out. She arrived shortly after—with wine. Was she trying to ensure I got her drunk so the rape would be easier to achieve? Obviously not. This meant she did not think any of this at the time.

She also implied that I knew no one else would join us. This was a lie. She seemed to accept that she hadn't known everyone else was going to the bar, so why did she find it inconceivable that I also had not known this at the time I asked if she wanted to come out? She was assuming. Also, if I was so hung up on her, then why did I remain outside without her or the others when she changed her mind and joined them inside? Even when they came out later, after the bar closed, I remained by myself, rather than seeking her out.

On that note, once I noticed she was giving off weird vibes to me, I left her alone, not approaching her for the next several days despite not understanding what had changed. Doesn't that show me as respecting wishes that I did not even understand? How does that make me a creep? That is what men are *supposed* to do if a woman who has made sexual remarks to them suddenly goes cold and distant, as if no longer interested. Of course, the other reason I had avoided her was my knowledge that she had bad-mouthed me.

She brought up our age difference. Well, my age hadn't changed (by more than a day or two anyway, and so had hers!) from when she thought these things were fine to when she thought they were creepy. She also said she liked older men. But she was right that depending on the age difference, some people—not all—think the romantic interest of older men is creepy. But that's another thing—I hadn't shown her *overtly* romantic interest, and certainly nothing on par with what she had been doing. The drinking and dinner invites could be seen that way out of context, but they were not explicitly so *in* context.

Part of me wondered if someone had stalked Emma, or assaulted in her past. It would explain her paranoia and seeing innocent actions in such sinister ways. But would such a woman think it's funny (and perfectly okay) that two strange men had asked for her bra on the street? Or that it's okay to repeatedly say she wants someone to grope her? Or to giggle about how she really wanted to eat a fergburger? At first glance, no, because she should know that she's condoning and inviting her objectification without regard for her personhood. But sexual assault victims, particularly when it happened at a young age, can show an excessive amount of interest in sexualized talk. I knew this from my own experience with it, and so I wondered. But even if it was true, it did not justify her accusations or behavior.

Texting me "I want us apart" is creepy.

I had told her in my apology that I would continue to keep apart from her. This apparently wasn't proof of respect or consideration as intended, but more proof I was a creep. I got the impression she believed that *I* thought we were in a romantic relationship with each other and my use of the word "apart" meant we were "taking a break" from that. If that was what I had meant, this would indeed have been creepy and "bizarre." She went on to ask that I leave her alone, even though I already had, and just said I was going to continue to do that. Did she think my intention to remain "apart" was temporary because I intended that we would soon resume our supposed relationship and she had to tell me to make being apart long term? How could she conclude this?

I only had one idea—I had shown thoughtfulness in suggesting to JJ that she alone be allowed to go on the dolphin encounter swim if it arose. This had nothing to do with her personally, but maybe she thought it did. There is no shortage of guys doing something nice for a girl, thinking she'll appreciate it and develop feelings for him. JJ had brought this up to me in his efforts to have me hook up with Emma, and his intention might have been obvious to her when informing her the idea had been mine.

She likely thought that an intention to cause feelings had been mine, and I had indeed briefly wondered if it was a good idea before realizing it was not too late to stop JJ. I had bought into this crap when younger, too, as Hollywood peddles it in countless films and shows. But it is typically wrong. People don't like it if you show seemingly romantic kindness when they do not feel that way about you. It is why someone having a crush on us is repulsive to most. It now seemed possible that this suggestion about the dolphin thing, coupled with my use of the word "apart," conjured in her mind that I believed myself to have an imagined relationship with her. And thus, had I become a creep. It was all fiction.

She seemed to think I had some sort of crush. I was a grown man, recently divorced and dating again after over sixteen years of marriage, and with two little kids at home. I was not some shy, awkward, horny teenager with limited life experience that led to romanticizing a girl instead of talking to her. Was Emma projecting her immaturity onto me?

...your behavior has made me extremely uncomfortable

She emphasized how uncomfortable I had supposedly made her. She was clearly oblivious to how uncomfortable she had made me, and quite a few others feel with her repeated "grope me" comments. While making someone feel that way by accident is not great, it happens, and it's not high on a list of offenses. It's certainly nowhere near as bad as her accusations, repeated behind my back to a bunch of people we were traveling with. And here I was being chastised by *that* person for making *her* uncomfortable.

She seemed to want sympathy from me (even though I had just expressed it) or to make me feel bad about how I had made her feel. But I wasn't exactly sympathetic anymore. I'm guessing she either hadn't known or didn't care that I knew she had badmouthed me to the others, or that she was now telling me what she had said. Did she care how she made *me* feel by doing so? Multiple people asked me if I was okay, and more of them likely saw my distress. Did she? Maybe. She wasn't terribly observant, including about her impact on people, but from the sheer hostility in her response, I am certain that if she had been aware of the upset she caused me, she would have rejoiced. This would say something about her, just as me giving an apology when I believed I had done nothing wrong had said something about me. Her "woe is me" schtick rang hollow.

Thank you for making me throw up on my mouth

Her parting words about my apology making her vomit in her mouth showed more commitment to the fantasy she had spun. I had been polite to her but, for reasons I did not yet understand, she retroactively saw it all as sinister and me purposefully making her feel fearful and "extremely uncomfortable." Viewed that way, my apology, casting myself as a good man who respected women, must have seemed not only grossly insincere but an insult to her intelligence, and a reversal of our roles. She fancied herself as a sweet, innocent maiden, and me as a creepy stalker and rapist. Given my obvious and unspeakable evil, how dare I apologize as if I have compassion, sensitivity, and good will? An expression of regret meant to ease her concerns had instead caused a volcano of fury to erupt.

No one is required to accept our apology, and given her fantasy, her horrific response no longer surprised me. Part of me thought Emma deserved to never receive another apology again for the rest of her life.

By the time I went to bed, my conscience was clear. I had done nothing wrong other than knocking on her door, but I'd had a justifiable reason. I thought very little of her. I didn't give a damn what she thought anymore. And if anyone else believed even a single part of whatever she had told them, that was their problem. They were all strangers I would never see again anyway. There would be no black cloud over my head.

Day 9 of 10

The next morning, I was in a great mood, having dramatically rebounded. The ability to do so was something that I still marveled at, because chronic depression had dominated two decades of my life and when you're in that state and something new upsets you, the impact lingers. But not anymore. I felt clearheaded, energized, and determined to enjoy the highlight of the trip, the one I had most looked forward to—a trip through giant, majestic mountains to Milford Sound and its waterfalls. My excitement had returned. We would return to our hotel that night, so with a day bag already packed, I joined the others outside to walk back to town for a buffet breakfast.

Figure 12 Mountains and Valleys

Emma wasn't present, to my relief, but part of me didn't care. I would skip nothing on account of her, make no adjustments. If I wanted to stand in a given spot for something like a photo and she was there, I would do so. I would do what I wanted, and she could move her crazy ass away if she didn't like it. She had ruined half my day yesterday, but I was determined she would have no further impact on me.

And so I felt great as I stood among them, my usual demeanor back to normal or even accentuated. I felt dimly aware that I was projecting an air of everything being okay again, but it wasn't a ruse. I just no longer needed anyone wondering if I was okay or checking in on me. I didn't want to be a black cloud over anyone else, including Emma, though in her case, I couldn't have cared less. But the others? I wanted them to know I was back. I still felt heartfelt appreciation for those who had showed concern for me in my silent distress. These were the kind of people I needed and wanted in my life. Part of me wanted to show my appreciation, and I had my first chance minutes later.

We walked across a park's lone path as a shortcut to the main strip of road that ended at the T-intersection, our buffet breakfast awaiting somewhere over there. I happened to be bringing up the rear alone when Paal suddenly fell in beside me, having been trying to catch up with us. I turned to him with a big smile.

"You'll never guess what Emma accused me of last night," I said.

A moment of surprise passed over his face before he laughed and clapped me on the back, already commiserating because she had previously victimized him. Did misery love company? From our instant bond over that single remark of mine, I knew it did. "Oh no, I can't imagine."

We only had a few minutes, so I gave him the short version about the sushi dinner invitation.

"Yeah, but you said that to everyone. Twice. I heard you."

"Right. And I didn't exactly fight it when she suggested asking the others. It's not like I said, 'Oh no baby, I want to get you alone. Just you and me. You're so beautiful.' It should have been obvious I was fine with them coming. I mean, what was I going to do, try to ditch them when they were ten feet away and approaching us? Wouldn't have worked even if that had been my intent."

"Right."

I then brought the groping thing and her interpretation. He shook his head.

"You know," he began, "I give you credit for actually telling her to stop it. I was thinking the same thing and I just never said it. I'm glad you had the balls."

I nodded my thanks, smiling. "Or the stupidity. I think I now know why you said nothing. You are smarter than me."

He companionably struck my arm with the back of one hand, laughing. "Well, you did the right thing. At least someone finally did. I'm really sorry she reacted that way. That's messed up."

"There's more, too." I told him about knocking on her door, her accepting that, and everything that followed, included overhearing her badmouthing me. I told him she had done the same thing to him in that exact spot the night before, before concluding, "After what she just did to me, I don't believe a word of what she said about you."

He again clapped me on the back in visible relief. "I swear I only made the one comment to her."

"I believe you. She has no credibility with me now."

"Is this what was bothering you last night?"

"Yeah."

"I'm just glad it was only this. I thought something had happened to your kids."

That surprised me. "No, I was just in shock." I admitted to having worried how many people she'd told this story to and who believed it, and he said he had heard no one talking about it and doubted anyone would have accepted it, it was too far "out there." I thanked him and we joked about trying to save each other from Evil Emma for the rest of the trip. We hung out a lot, often exchanging looks of amusement or disdain about something Emma said within earshot of us. Darlene frequently noticed this with an arched eyebrow, clearly wondering about a shared joke she wasn't in on, but before long, she understood and smiled knowingly.

Emma arrived late to breakfast, initially taking a seat only one spot removed from me at our six-person table. Really? But then others also came late while she was at the buffet and she moved herself, to my relief, Paal and I chuckling about it. We soon boarded the bus for a ride through the valleys, with occasional stops for pictures. I had waited for this more than anything else and felt at home among the towering monoliths of gray stone, though only a few had snow atop them. Eye candy for the soul loomed around me. I wished we could stay longer to watch the shadows changing with the hours, but the overcast sky prevented rays of sun from doing their magic among the peaks. I enjoyed it anyway and felt the highlights were living up to expectations.

We arrived at the gorgeous Milford Sound for our double-decker ferry ride, the best of the trip coming last and not disappointing. All around the water's edge stood mountains that rose right from the shore without a trace of beach. No matter where one looked, a waterfall plunged down cliffs and into the still waters, mist churning into a breeze, moody clouds above. Only the briefness of our visit marred the experience, but the determination to squeeze every ounce of enjoyment kept me on the upper deck long after everyone else went below for sandwiches. They did these even as we neared the most picturesque waterfall, which plunged from a valley formed by two adjacent peaks. I couldn't imagine how good the sandwiches must be for everyone to not remain on deck just as we reached the optimal viewing point. The result was that I was the last to come down and ended up alone at a booth. Directly behind me sat Darlene, who at one point leaned back and looked at me.

"You doing okay?" she asked.

"I am doing *great*," I replied. Since I didn't want her to take my word for it, and she had now twice asked how I was doing, and I wanted a woman's opinion on all of it, I added, "Ready to talk if you still want to listen. No worries if not."

"I'll be right there!" Darlene finished up with her friend, who left, and scooted into my booth across from me.

I started giving her the light rundown. She agreed that there was nothing odd about the sushi place invite. And when I brought up the groping subject and what I had said to Emma, she suddenly got animated.

"Oh my God, Rand," she started, "she's like 29 going on 19. Women do not say that shit about wanting to be groped. It was funny for five minutes, but after that? She's fucking stupid." I started laughing, loving her bluntness. "I'm serious."

"You don't think I threatened to do it?"

She gave me an amused, withering look. "Please. I can read you better than that."

"You frighten me a little," I joked.

She grinned. "No, I don't."

I moved on to the subject of how I knew where Emma's room was in Kaikoura and why I knocked on Emma's door instead of reaching out via WhatsApp, and she interrupted me.

"Let me stop you right there. Yes, knocking on the door of a single woman will make her uncomfortable."

"Yeah, I figured that one out."

"I'm not saying you did anything wrong, but that is the way it is. Now you know."

"Yeah."

"But the rest of that shit about you stalking her? That's fucked up. There's no way, like you could even do that without the rest of us noticing." As I laughed, she added, "I could tell you were interested in her. So was Paal, but you know what? She was interested in you, too. And she acted like it. All that time saying in front of you that she wanted to be groped? That was some lame ass flirting."

"I thought only guys did it that badly."

"Nah. Dumb ass girls do it, too. I've seen that shit before when I was that young. People say stupid shit."

We talked more and somehow the moment last night, when I had walked past where they were eating and they called out to me, came up, and she smiled. "You heard us calling your name, didn't you?"

I laughed. There was no putting anything past her. "Yeah, I just needed to be alone."

"I knew it! I thought, 'There's no way he didn't hear us.'"

When I brought up the subject of inviting Emma to come out and drink again, she jumped in once more. "There is nothing wrong with asking someone to have drinks with you. I don't agree with her at all, but I will tell you this—she was leading both you and Paal on. You don't play pool alone with a guy, or have drinks with him, if you are not interested. It sends a message, and you both got the right one. That she changed her mind is fine, but what she said afterward is fucked up. And we talked to her about this."

My eyebrows rose. "What? You did?"

"Yeah. She was badmouthing you and Paal to a bunch of us and we were all over that shit. I told her that if she's not interested, to act like it, and don't give mixed signals. A bunch of us told her she was full of shit and to knock it off if she didn't like you guys getting interested in her."

I settled back into the chair, vastly relieved. Emma had indeed talked shit about me, and Paal, and the rest of the women hadn't believed a word of it. Instead, they had criticized her and told her it was her own damn fault. That helped explain why no one had commented on her accusations to me, when word had reached Paal's ears about her badmouthing him prior to that. This implied people believed what she'd said about him, but it's speculation. Then again, Emma's remarks about Paal were so much less loaded than what she accused me of. Had she overplayed her attempt to vilify me and had it blow up in her face because people sensed I would not stalk and threaten to grope her? Probably. I would like to think so anyway.

I almost wanted to kiss Darlene for this revelation, except that would make me a creep, of course. Now I wished I had talked to her the day before! I had told myself I didn't care what anyone thought of me anymore, but part of me had known I was kidding myself. The talk with Darlene was a welcome surprise that had me buoyant afterward. Every time I saw Emma, I grinned.

And I now suspected what had really happened. I think Emma did revisionist history about our supposed incidents in Kaikoura, and the talk with Darlene and the others triggered it. When I told Emma to stop saying she wanted to be groped because someone might do it, I challenged her judgment about what was appropriate. She clearly thought saying that was okay, and I told her otherwise. This likely made her uncomfortable and embarrassed. What if I was right? Then she had been foolish in front of the entire group. This undoubtedly made her feel bad. Had it eaten away at her?

What I think happened was that after my comment, Emma sought support from the other women. Instead of being told her behavior was okay, easing the insecurity I had triggered, the others told her in no uncertain times that this was indeed as bad as I had suggested, maybe even worse. That she was a fool. That she was leading me and Paal on. That she was inviting sexual assault. That over and over again, her judgment was wrong. Emma had sought support and got a giant smack down instead, from other women no less.

Who was to blame for this? Emma, of course, but people rarely accept responsibility for their actions. Emma blamed me. After all, I was the first person to tell her the groping stuff was bad, setting in motion a chain reaction to that smack down. All of it likely made her feel embarrassed, ashamed, humiliated—and "extremely uncomfortable" about her past behavior and maybe even how she was supposed to act from now on. Did this explain her looking lost and despondent while standing away from everyone when we arrived at Queenstown's airport the next day?

In the end, her attack on me was a defense of herself. I had indeed threatened and attacked her without meaning to. Not physically, but psychologically, emotionally, and even socially, which helps explain her retaliating the same way. The strength of her accusations mirrored the strength of her humiliation. It also reflected the fury that my apology caused.

She was three days into rebuilding her self-esteem, trying to reject the feedback about her behavior and what it implied about her—that she was reckless, foolish, immature, and stupid. She was reasserting her previous narrative—she was a good person, and her behavior was fine and could be continued despite the feedback, letting her become comfortable once more. Did that explain her later returning to sexualized jokes, this time about fergburgers?

Someone else was the bad guy. That was obviously me because I had made her feel bad about herself, something only a jerk would do. Days later, I threatened her narrative by apologizing, something only a good, considerate, thoughtful person does. Accepting my apology meant accepting the narrative that had humiliated her. She had to respond instantly and forcefully that I was a jerk and *she* was the good one. Of course, I had no way of knowing all of this was going on in her head.

While the experience was very negative, part of me was glad for it because I learned a few things; I would rather learn with less upset, but such is life. I now know that it doesn't matter why I'm knocking on a woman's door unexpectedly. I'm just not going to do it unless the place is burning down. The risk isn't worth it. I also have to stop assuming people will view things in a positive light and do more to ward off a misunderstanding by being explicit. In this case, that would mean specifying I would like others to join us when I confirmed she wanted to do something with me again. On the other hand, being ambiguous provides a low-confrontation way of gauging someone's interest, and this is valuable and should not result in accusations. There's no reason a woman can't make it clear she is not interested without attacking you.

As for the groping warning I gave her, part of me wants to say I wouldn't do it again, that her getting herself attacked is not my problem, but I would because I believe it's the right thing to do. Someone setting themselves up for sexual assault is not something I can turn a blind eye to. Maybe next time I would warn her with witnesses and be more explicit. I overestimated Evil Emma's good qualities and underestimated her nasty ones. I have an unfortunate tendency to assume the best of other, some of whom have the opposite trait of assuming the worst about me.

I had already noticed on the way to Milford Sound that Emma seemed happy, even giddy, and in the best mood I had seen her. I had designed my apology to make her feel comfortable again, and I smirked to myself that it had worked. Not the apology itself, of course, but her unloading days' worth of bad feelings on me. I felt only amusement about her, partly because it was I, not her, who had enjoyed the group's benefit of the doubt. Oh, how the tables had turned.

The dark whisperer in Emma had told her things that were not true, then made her whisper them to others. And no one had believed. This isn't the way to fill the self with light, by putting your darkness into others, and for those that feel it works, they are much of what is wrong with "the world." Being a good person is not part of the problem, but the solution to many of life's troubles, and I felt fortunate that the lone dark whisperer in my midst could not duplicate herself in those around me. They had not succumbed to be like her. Neither had I save for a night of trying to understand, and that it was good people do. I may not have been a saint, but I was no evil figure. Emma had taken that spot for herself, her fears, insecurities, and other all-too-human failings leading her to act horrendously. We do not have to give in to them and take them out on others. That is the difference between good and evil.

Our ferry returned to the best of the waterfalls, which we had seen from a long distance before. This time, we pulled right up into the mist at its best, getting wet as we jostled for position at the boat's bow and taking photos. Green plants clung to the cliff face, swaying in the rush of air from the falls. The roaring sound of falling water surrounded me. Only at its base could I feel so tiny compared to this force of nature. And I knew the trip would get no better now. I felt glad I had come and only wished to re-peat it all and take more time and the places of greatest interest to me.

My jubilation culminated that night as the group had a final gathering on our last night together, in Te Anau. They wanted to visit the place I had eaten dinner at alone the night before in my distress, the one with live music and a lone pool table. As we bought beers and mingled, I went to the pool table, trying to figure out how we could purchase a game or two. Paal saw and joined me, and soon we were playing. The rest of the group gathered around because it provided something to watch, at least, as a band tore through modern hits nearby. Our driver, Kent, arrived and started a game against us with Tom, with two locals soon deciding to play the winner of every round. I joked to my-self that I wanted to ask the band to play "Creep" by Radi-ohead and have them dedicate it to Emma, from me and Paal.

Figure 13 The Waterfall

As the night went on, I noticed that there was no longer any sign of Emma. When I mentioned this to Paal, we both laughed. It was fitting. The woman who had tried to turn the group against both of us was nowhere to be seen on our last night of partying together, because that party had ended up revolving around the two men she had falsely accused of undue attention on her. Let her go sit alone in her room, wondering what others were saying about her. She deserved it. And Paal and I deserved to be the center of positive attention from the same group of people. We were having a blast.

Day 10

The next day, Kent drove us several hours back to Queenstown and the airport where most of us said our goodbyes. Some of us had similar flights out to connecting legs, whether to Australia, Auckland, or beyond. I was headed to Wellington on the north island to see another major city.

Once on my plane, I breathed a sigh of relief to be away from Emma and everyone else. I have often been a loner, and while I had enjoyed being social on the trip, I wanted some alone time. Having no one planning activities for me brought some freedom but responsibility. In that sense, some of my vacation—the part where I didn't need to think for myself—was over. Traveling to a foreign country alone for the first time can also cause apprehension, though without a language barrier, this was less of a concern. But now that I had been in New Zealand for nearly two weeks, I knew what to expect.

Except for Emma's antics, I had enjoyed the trip so far, with Queenstown and Kaikoura the clear favorites aside from Milford Sound. But I felt no compulsion to visit Kaikoura again. I only experienced a fraction of Queenstown's adventures would love to spend a week or more there, including experiencing more of the culture. Though it's a small place, it has city-like elements amid a beautiful, rural landscape, making it nearly ideal for me. I have often wanted to rent an RV in the United States and just go sightseeing and could see doing it on New Zealand's South Island.

Once at the Wellington airport, I hailed an Uber for a ride through the city to my hilltop hotel, the best accommodations I enjoyed so far. The driver took the long way by the coastline to show me around a bit as we exchanged stories. I didn't mind. What's a few extra bucks on a $5000 trip? I'm normally more into landscape sightseeing, but everything from architecture to street signs and vehicles are often quite different in another country. Nothing noteworthy stood out, however, but then I was just passing through. I gave him a good tip for the experience.

But for only the second time on vacation, it rained that night so that I spent most of it in my room, enjoying solitude and watching local news, something I hadn't done yet. This proved a good way to learn more about a culture, and I regretted not doing it sooner. The weather report, which they did for the entire country, kept my interest far more than I would have expected because I did not know what the weather patterns were—I am apparently a bit of a geek. I had a city bus tour scheduled the next morning, checking out but leaving my bags at the front desk. I purposely left behind "George," my huge chunk of cheese, which few had helped me with; I was sick of eating it, and only now was I truly on my own!

The tour bus picked me up at the hotel, something they did for most on the hours-long trip. We visited an historic church, a red cable car that carried us up part of a large hill, a botanical garden, and a city/harbor overlook. While most of it failed to excite, I used this to be driven around town and hear various tidbits about Wellington. The bus door broke at one point, forcing us to wait for a replacement vehicle that improved our ride. Fortunately, this did not affect my next activity after a quick walk around town while eating a sandwich. I took another bus tour to visit the Weta Workshop, the studios responsible for many special effects for *The Lord of the Rings* and more. I learned how they make props, including those for actors who are over six feel tall when they are playing a dwarf on film. I left Wellington glad I had taken a day to get an initial feel, even though this isn't nearly long enough.

Then I flew to Auckland to see the capital, which was the first place that reminded me of a major U.S. city for its size and modernity. But my accommodations were the worst this time, dirty, poor quality, and sometimes just odd, such as having to enter through a bar/restaurant. My next city tour didn't go as planned when I walked to the harbor to meet at a Maori statue and the tour operator never showed. Or so I thought. With no phone or Wi-Fi service, I walked around to see if I had misunderstood the meeting location and that a second statue existed. I also hoped to find free Wi-Fi to no avail. In doing this, I apparently stepped away when he finally arrived twenty minutes late, didn't wait long for me, and departed without me by the time I returned. Not knowing this, I walked back to the hotel for the internet and exchanged some tense emails with him, where he claimed I was the no-show. I had to argue with him to get my refund.

On my own to salvage something for my last day, I went up the thousand-foot-tall Sky Tower, the second tallest freestanding building in the southern hemisphere, for a 360 look at Auckland. I lucked out when leaving, as the tourist attraction had hop-on, hop-off bus tours leaving from its base. I snagged one with just enough time to get a feel for the metropolis before my flights home, but with that worrying me a little, I only got off twice. I hoped to return one day, but for now, disappointment mixed with resignation - I just wanted to go home, but a concern loomed as I caught another bus to the airport.

Figure 14 At the Weta Workshop

Back when Emma and I were still talking, we had learned that we had the same flight back to the United States from Auckland. I couldn't know if she remembered, but I did and wanted no part of this. But I wasn't changing my multi-leg flight, having carefully planned everything. She was like a black cloud that I didn't want hanging over me, a sinister, unpredictable force of psychological lunacy.

At the airport, I couldn't help scanning my surroundings for Emma, relieved to not see her. In the boarding area, I first looked at every face to make sure she wasn't there. Then I took a seat that allowed me to see everyone else who gathered for the flight as they arrived. As the minutes ticked by, there was no sign of my nemesis, but I knew that could change anytime. I continued checking out new arrivals as I boarded and took my seat, the plane just small enough that I could see she wasn't already on it, my seat allowing me to see each new passenger as they boarded. I wouldn't quite say I was holding my breath, but not until the plane door closed did I relax. Whether or not it had anything to do with me, and I suspected it did, Emma had changed her flight. I never saw her again.

Thank God for small miracles.

About the Author

Randy Zinn is a proud father to a son (b. 2012) and daughter (b. 2016) and loves spending time with them when not writing memoirs, making music, playing golf, or lap swimming. Under another name, he's published non-fiction and fantasy stories with a literary bent, and released several albums of his music (hard rock and acoustic guitar). He holds a Bachelor of Music in classical guitar, Magna cum Laude, and has worked as a software developer/architect in the Washington D.C. area for over 20 years as an employee, contractor, or consultant through his own company.

He's also faced a variety of personal issues, including Attention Deficit Disorder, speech problems, sexual assaults, depression, suicide, bullying, being Learning Disabled, and a devastating injury, all of which he overcame. The tales in his memoirs cover them all and his dramatic, life-changing transformation.

Connect with me online

http://www.Randy-Zinn.com
https://www.facebook.com/pg/randyzinnauthor
http://bit.ly/ZinnAmazon

If you like this book, please help others enjoy it.

Lend it. Please share this book with others.

Recommend it. Please recommend it to friends, family, reader groups, and discussion boards

Review it. Please review the book at Goodreads and the vendor where you bought it.

JOIN THE RANDY ZINN NEWSLETTER!

Subscribers receive the latest updates, the chance to join the ARC Team, and bonus content like deleted scenes, short stories, private/color photos, and priority access to learn more from Rand about what interest you.

http://www.randy-zinn.com/newsletter

Randy Zinn Books

Memoirs

A Storm of Lies
Corporate Hell: A Memoir
Consulting Hell: A Memoir

A Silence Not So Golden Trilogy
Book 1: *Refusal to Engage: My Voice is Become Death*
Book 2: *A Blast of Light: My Rebirth Through Music*
Book 3: *The Wine-Dark Sea: My New Life Awaits*

The Memoir Shorts
Book 1: *Adventures in Opposite Land*
Book 2: *Am I Evil?*

CPSIA information can be obtained
at www.ICGtesting.com
Printed in the USA
BVHW032129030521
606358BV00006B/45